A WORLD DIVIDED

Dedicated to the memory of

E P Thompson

writer, historian and peace campaigner

died 28 August, 1993

A WORLD DIVIDED

Militarism and Development After the Cold War

Edited by Geoff and Kath Tansey and Paul Rogers

St. Martin's Press
New York

© Geoff Tansey and Paul Rogers, 1994

All rights reserved. For information, write:
Scholarly and Reference Division,
St. Martin's Press, 175 Fifth Avenue,
New York, NY 10010

First published in the United States of America in 1994

Printed and bound in Great Britain by
Clays Ltd, St Ives plc

ISBN 0-312-12350-7

Library of Congress Cataloging in Publication Data applied for.

Contents

Notes on the Contributors

Paul Rogers is Professor of Peace Studies and head of the Department of Peace Studies at the University of Bradford.

Frances Stewart is director of Queen Elizabeth House, University of Oxford and **Ken Wilson** is on leave from QEH working with the Ford Foundation in Mozambique.

Nadir Abdel Latif Mohammed was MacArthur Post-Doctoral Research Fellow, The Global Security Programme, Faculty of Social and Political Sciences, University of Cambridge at the time of the seminar in July 1993. He has since moved to the Centre for the Study of African Economies, Institute of Economics and Statistics, University of Oxford.

Steve Schofield is co-director of the Project on Demilitarization (Prodem), 20 Central Road, Leeds.

Ben Jackson is the campaigns coordinator of the World Development Movement, London.

Geoff Tansey is a freelance writer and consultant and co-convenor, with Paul Rogers, of the Development, Disarmament and Security Study Group of the Development Studies Association.

Kathleen Tansey is a freelance writer and editor and has also taught science and English as a Foreign Language.

Preface

Picture a luxury hotel in the midst of poverty, adjacent to a squatter camp and surrounded by high wire fences and with armed guards at the entrance. Some guests do not notice, and simply enjoy the facilities, others feel uncomfortable yet accept that it is just the way it is; and still others know that this is not the way to live. In July 1993, when Paul Rogers went to an international workshop in South Asia on environment and development that is the situation he found himself in. It seemed like a metaphor for our whole world — one which many of those looking forward in fiction (and in think tanks) portray as a nasty, brutish place for many, with comfort and privilege secured behind various kinds of barriers for a few.

That is not a developed world, but a divided one. And it is one we want to avoid. It holds not joy and happiness for our children and children's children, but distress and danger. To avoid these gloomy scenarios requires action on a scale humankind usually reserves for war making, not peace building.

Yet times of change, of danger, are also times of great opportunity. We live in such times now, with the Cold War barriers destroyed and other barriers yet to be constructed. The foundations for these have been laid, however, and they could divert humankind into further destruction. The dangers are of a shift from the East–West confrontation of the past 40 years to a North-South one. In fact, the East–West confrontation was something of a side show from the *real* divisions in the world. But divisions can be healed; even in the midst of conflict steps can be taken both to minimize its effects and seek ways out of it. That is what we are concerned with in this book. We want to understand the realities of the present, the impact of war on human development, and ways of minimizing and avoiding these. Our human response to differences of interest needs to be not one that seeks to overcome them violently but to resolve them peacefully.

This book came out of a workshop on Militarism and Development held in London on 2 July 1993, which was organized jointly by the

Development, Disarmament and Security Study Group of the Development Studies Association (DSA),* the World Development Movement (WDM) and the Department of Peace Studies at the University of Bradford. It drew together both academics and activists from development non-governmental organizations (ngos). The papers presented brought together a range of perspectives that could contribute to promoting public debate about avoiding what we can see emerging – *a world divided*. This requires both new thinking and an openness to crossing traditional intellectual, economic, activist and other boundaries.

The contributors revised, and we have edited, the initial papers in the light of the discussions at the meeting. The concluding chapter draws on the various discussions to outline some key issues that should be tackled at various levels – from local to global. We hope this book will appeal to a wide audience – from ordinary citizens concerned about building a better world to academics in a range of disciplines, activists in environmental, development and peace ngos, and policy makers in governments and corporations.

Geoff and Kathleen Tansey
November 1993

---

* Further information about the study group can be had from Geoff Tansey or Paul Rogers, c/o Department of Peace Studies, University of Bradford, West Yorkshire BD7 1DP, UK.

Acknowledgements

We are grateful to the Joseph Rowntree Charitable Trust for its support for the editorial work required to take the issues discussed at this small workshop to a much wider audience through production of this book. We also thank the DSA for the support provided to the Development, Disarmament and Security Study Group, to WDM for its work in organizing the workshop in London and to the Department of Peace Studies at the University of Bradford for its support.

Glossary

ADI	Air Defence Initiative
ALCM	Air-Launched Cruise Missile
ARPA	Advanced Research Projects Agency
ATACMS	Army Tactical Missile System
CENTCOM	Central Command (US)
CFSP	Common Foreign and Security Policy
CIA	Central Intelligence Agency
CIIR	Catholic Institute for International Relations
DESO	Defence Export Sales Organization (UK)
DoD	Department of Defense (Pentagon) (US)
DoE	Department of Energy (US)
DSA	Development Studies Association
DTI	Department of Trade and Industry (UK)
EC	European Community
ECGD	Export Credit Guarantee Department
EMP	Electromagnetic Pulse
EU	European Union, name adopted by EC from November 1993 when the Maastricht Treaty took effect
GATT	General Agreement on Tariffs and Trade
GDP	Gross Domestic Product
GNP	Gross National Product
IFAD	International Fund for Agricultural Development
IMF	International Monetary Fund
INF	Intermediate-Range Nuclear Forces
MoD	Ministry of Defence (UK)
NATO	North Atlantic Treaty Organization
ngo	non-governmental organization
ODA	Overseas Development Administration
OEA	Office of Economic Adjustment (US)
OST	Office of Science and Technology (UK)
OTA	Office of Technology Assessment (US)
RAF	Royal Air Force (UK)
R&D	Research and Development
RDF	Rapid Deployment Force
RRE	Royal Radar Establishment
SDI	Strategic Defence Initiative
SIPRI	Stockholm International Peace Research Institute
START	Strategic Arms Reduction Treaty
TGWU	Transport and General Workers Union (UK)
THAAD	Theatre High Altitude Area Defence
UN	United Nations

UNDP	United Nations Development Programme
UNICEF	United Nations Children's Fund
UNEP	United Nations Environment Programme
USAF	United States Air Force
WCED	World Commission on Environment and Development
WDM	World Development Movement

Introduction

Maria Elena Hurtado

For me, nothing underlined better the need to sharpen the voices that speak for a more egalitarian, less divided, world – a world organized around agreed international rules and values – than the midnight raid on Baghdad on 26 June 1993. My first reaction to the news that the USA had rained cruise missiles on Baghdad was one of utter indignation, of rage against cowboy politics. Give a cowboy high-tech guns and there won't be any security in town – even if the cowboy tells you that he is the sheriff!

This is even truer now that we no longer have the restraining powers of the former Soviet Union either on the ground or in the UN Security Council. Because restraints are so weak, we may be in for high-tech forms of gunboat diplomacy. High-tech gunboat diplomacy allows an exercise of power which costs the superpowerful very little; they will not even have to go through the shock of witnessing their victims – often children – being blown to pieces.

Humankind has mastered the universe but has signally failed to learn how to live in peace and harmony with its other fellow human beings, and with nature. As the former director of Friends of the Earth, David Gee, likes to say, we proudly call ourselves *Homo Sapiens* when *Homo stupidus* would be a more accurate description of our totally irrational behaviour.

Security can never be achieved by arming ourselves to the teeth, which then encourages our neighbours to do the same, setting up a vicious upward spiral of arms spending and destruction. At the World Development Movement (WDM), we have been talking for some time of the concept of 'real security'. Real security is achieved through security from hunger, security from disease, repression, poverty, and environmental collapse. Real security was the theme of our autumn 1993 campaign, which emphasized the links between human development, environmental sustainability, disarmament and peace. Ben Jackson's paper – a revised version of a WDM publication – explores these links and the changes needed in the North to secure a safer world. Ordinary people still do not realize how the abject poverty suffered by millions is the other face of the affluence enjoyed by a few.

With the Cold War ended, any justification (however spurious) for the need to build up nuclear weapons as a deterrent has gone. Eliminating nuclear weapons is obviously a key part of real security. WDM supports the appeal for a nuclear test ban for at least three reasons: first, because an end to testing would over time lead towards the elimination of nuclear weapons; secondly, because it is obscene to spend so much money on these instruments of death while so many of our fellow human beings live in absolute poverty and insecurity; and thirdly, because nuclear testing – and its effects – has been foisted on people who had no choice in the matter, for example in Australia and the South Pacific.

The true source of insecurity is the insecurity of people. Indeed, Third World development is at the core of the UN agenda for peace. UN Secretary-General Boutros Boutros Ghali has stated that peace and prosperity are indivisible because economic hardship and social disintegration are both causes and consequences of violence and war.

Inflation has been low in developed countries in the 1980s largely due to the collapse of commodity prices. From the collapse of coffee prices alone, Africa has lost in the past three years more than all the net aid of the World Bank to all African countries south of the Sahara. Such sharp shocks undoubtedly create instability. In Colombia, the collapse of the coffee agreement led to violence in coffee-growing areas and to more planting of coca, the raw material for cocaine.

While there is no doubt that poverty breeds instability, conflict and wars, there are other forces of insecurity at work that are even more difficult to address, if that is possible, because they seem to be lodged deep within human nature. I am referring to our Western culture of individualism, of every man and woman for himself or herself, and its group version – every ethnic group for itself, every religion competing against all other religions. I must confess that when we at WDM trace insecurity to economic, social and environmental stress, I always hope that I am not asked how do I explain the tragedy of former Yugoslavia or the ethnic conflicts between Sikhs and Hindus in India. Of course I can answer that the problems of maintaining political stability and furthering democracy in South Asia, for example, are made more difficult by massive economic and demographic pressures. The region accounts for just two per cent of global income but has to feed 22 per cent of the global population. Almost half its people live below the poverty line and its population is increasing by 25 million a year – five times faster than in the industrial countries.

But economic strictures are only part of the answer. Indeed I believe that real security will only be attained when secular, democratic and pluralistic values take root in every corner of the earth, and, I would add, secular values in the sense of a strict separation between state and religion while at the same time guaranteeing full freedom of religions and conscience. A signal failure of people like us has been our inability to expand those values fast and wide enough. I am not talking here only of the imperialist Serbs or the arrogant leaders of the US. The ideologies of narrow populist nationalism, of exclusion of others and of intolerance are flourishing on our very doorstep. Witness the way Europe is building walls against refugees and migrants or initiating creeping protectionism against the successful exporting countries of Asia.

Neelan Tiruchelvam of the International Centre for Ethnic Studies in Sri Lanka sees a link between ethnic rivalries and religious intolerance and the cultural individualism of our capitalist, Western culture. He compares this with the communitarian conceptions of justice, and conciliatory and consensual approaches to the resolution of conflict prevailing in the Hindu-Buddhist tradition, which includes such things as the obligation of reciprocity and mutual support within the family.

It is not clear to me that lasting peace and security can be based on a value system which puts the individual and all his or her whims and wishes centre-stage. There must also be sharing rather than selfishness, equality rather than exploitation and control by the strongest, negotiation rather than warfare and retaliation by 'surgical' strikes, and shared international rules of coexistence between nations and peoples.

In a way, we are in an ideal situation to move towards real security by reaping the peace dividend after the end of the Cold War. The UN has estimated that if industrial countries cut military spending by at least three per cent a year, this would release over US$ *one thousand billion* by the year 2000 for social spending at home and would also pay for a doubling of aid to the Third World.* Third World countries must also reap the peace dividend and cut military spending, which requires the arms pushers in Britain and other countries to stop their hard sell.

---

* UNDP (1992) Human Development Report 1992, New York and Oxford, OUP, p 9

Maria Elena Hurtado

Our task in the workshop was to start to put flesh into these concepts. It was rewarding to have ngos and academics from different constituencies putting their minds together on what we know, what we need to find out and what we need to do to achieve 'real security'. But it must spread far beyond this small group and produce ideas for concrete action that are visionary but that are also supported by sound, convincing facts, figures and arguments. Perhaps even more importantly, they must also be politically 'saleable' to ordinary citizens and enlightened politicians of all political hues. We need the facts, we need the rigorous analysis, we need the figures, but this will be just an intellectual game if we are not able to translate it into a credible political campaign. This is our task. Over to you.*

* Readers wanting to find out more about WDM or to join should contact WDM, 25 Beehive Place, London, SW9 7QR. Tel: 071 737 6215; Fax 071 274 8232

1

A Jungle Full of Snakes? Power, Poverty and International Security

Paul Rogers

Global security issues were dominated for 45 years by the ideological, economic and military confrontation between the superpowers. While this did not involve an all-out war between them, most of the 100 or more major conflicts which took place between 1945 and 1993 had an East–West dimension. The great majority of these were fought in the South and most of the 20 million people killed and 50 million people injured were their citizens.

The East–West confrontation was so great that by the end of the Cold War, 83 per cent of world annual military spending of $1000 billion was by the NATO and Warsaw Treaty alliances. They were also at the forefront of military research, development and deployments. Most NATO states spent at least ten times as much on the military as on international development and in the latter stages of the Cold War, after 1978, defence budgets grew as aid budgets fell.

With the ending of the East–West confrontation around 1989–91, military spending by the former Warsaw Pact nations fell rapidly, but that of the NATO member states was much slower to fall.[1] While there was a slight overall decrease in world military spending, the peace dividend in the West was minimal and there were even increases in military spending in some regions, especially the Middle East and South-East Asia.

Western strategists began to redefine what they thought their future security interests would be. They embraced new threats and problems, many of them originating beyond the old East–West divide, and often related to a new North–South axis of confrontation. As US President Clinton's newly appointed Director of the CIA put it, early in 1993, 'we have slain the dragon but now live in a jungle full of poisonous snakes'.[2]

This chapter reviews the main factors which are likely to dictate world security issues over the coming decades. This paints a radically different picture from that of the Cold War, with its ideological divisions and rigidly entrenched military strategies. Secondly, it examines some of the current trends in western security thinking, particularly in the US, and how these could actually increase the risks of North–South confrontation. Finally it suggests other, more appropriate, responses to these issues which are more likely to avoid conflict and enhance the chances of peace and international cooperation.[3]

GLOBAL SECURITY – FUTURE CAUSES OF CONFLICT

Three factors seem likely to influence trends in international peace and security around and beyond the turn of the century. The first factor is the deep polarization of the world's population into small areas of relative wealth and much larger areas of relative poverty. The distribution is not clear-cut, for there is deep poverty, deprivation and exploitation in many so-called rich states. In the US around 40 million people live below the poverty line, and in Britain there is severe poverty in every major urban area and clear evidence that the gap between rich and poor is growing wider.

Even so, the global picture overshadows these problems. Just one-fifth of the entire global population uses around three-quarters of the world's wealth and physical resources. This division is largely along geographical lines – traditionally termed First and Third Worlds or North and South. This polarization alone is a source of potential instability, which is seen most graphically in incidents of mass migration such as those common around Europe and North America in recent years, especially across the US-Mexican border and into Southern Europe.

This wealth-poverty polarization is steadily sharpening because the wealthy regions have already passed through the demographic transition and their populations are relatively stable while the populations of the

South are likely to grow for at least the next 60 years. In barely half that time, only one-seventh of the world's population will control at least three-quarters of the world's wealth. Pressures on those 'islands of wealth' will grow ever stronger.

A crisis of unsatisfied expectations might be avoided if prospects for international development were greater, but all the signs are that it will be slow and tortuous. Development is hindered not just by severe historic and continuing trading disadvantages but by a continuing debt crisis, economic exploitation and political instability. The numbers of people living in absolute poverty and suffering malnutrition have actually increased substantially in the past two decades. At the time of the severe international food crisis in 1974, some 450 million people world-wide were estimated to be malnourished. Twenty years later, over 780 million did 'not have enough food to meet their basic bodily needs for energy and protein'.[4] Although some progress in development has been made, largely from within the South, we have to assume that the massive disparities in global wealth and poverty will increase. The northern states, which still exert control over the world economy, show little commitment to cooperative international developments – hardly surprising since that very control is so advantageous to them.

The second factor which endangers our future security is that the entire global system appears to be approaching limits for human activity set by environmental constraints. At a regional level, these include immense problems of deforestation, water shortages, desertification, salinization and atmospheric and marine pollution. In the past 25 years, the world has lost over 400 million acres of tree cover (equal to the land area of the US to the east of the Mississippi River); deserts have grown by over 250 million acres (greater than the entire crop lands of China) and 480 billion tons of topsoil have been lost (equal to the crop lands of India)[5] Globally, environmental problems already include ozone depletion and global warming. Competition for resources is also intensifying, especially for those strategic resources such as oil which are now found predominantly in the South but consumed primarily in the North. On occasions, as in the Gulf in 1991, this competition results in open warfare.

Thirdly, we are faced with the primary legacy of the Cold War – world-wide militarization. Although the excesses of military confrontation are past, they leave behind a massive array of weapons, postures and attitudes, many of them searching for new 'threats' to provide further roles at a time of declining defence budgets.

The global phenomenon of ecological limits to growth is the result almost entirely of the activities of that minority of the world's population which is industrialized and maintains a high material standard of living. It now seems intent on maintaining that life-style at the expense of the economic prospects of most of the world's population. The majority will not find that acceptable, any more than the imposition of a 'new world order' along lines decreed by a minority of states acting with local elites, will be acceptable.

Recognition of this problem is not new – it was a feature of the 'Limits to Growth' debate of the early 1970s. The problem was put succinctly by the British ecologist, Palmer Newbould, writing shortly after the 1972 Human Environment Conference in Stockholm:

> My own belief is that however successful population policies are, the world population is likely to treble before it reaches stability. If the expectation of this increased population were, for example, to emulate the present lifestyle and resource use of the USA, the demand on world resources would be increased approximately 15-fold; pollution and other forms of environmental degradation might increase similarly and global ecological carrying capacity would then be seriously exceeded. There are therefore global constraints on development set by resources and environment and these will require a reduction in the per caput resource use and environmental abuse of the developed nations to accompany the increased resource use of the developing nations, a levelling down as well as up. This conflict cannot be avoided.[6]

Unless there were a change in political and economic outlook, the end result of the growing pressures of human demands would, according to Edwin Brooks, writing 20 years ago, result in a 'crowded, glowering planet of massive inequalities of wealth buttressed by stark force and endlessly threatened by desperate people in the global ghettoes of the under-privileged'.[7]

In essence then, a combination of grossly unequal distribution of wealth, with a crisis in development, progressive militarization and environmental limits to human activity make it probable that the dominant risk to global security in the next few decades will lie on a North–South axis of confrontation. This is likely to express itself in four main ways:

1. in conflicts over resources;
2. in migration;
3. in economic competition; and
4. through increasing responses from the South.

Resources

There will be a tendency towards conflict over the political control of strategic resources. Oil may be the most important but strategic minerals, food reserves and water resources will also figure prominently.

With Western Europe, Japan and now, crucially, the US, largely dependent for continued industrial performance on imported strategic resources, controlling access to those resources is already seen as a legitimate security concern. To the producers of these resources, this leads to a fear of a new hegemony rather than a peaceful new world order.

The Middle East will be the region of greatest potential competition for physical resources, with its remarkable concentration of oil reserves, especially with the steady depletion of oil reserves in the North. The Persian Gulf states now control two-thirds of all the world's oil reserves, and an even greater share of the easily-exploited reserves. Kuwait alone has three times as much oil as the entire US, including the oilfields of Alaska and the offshore reserves of the Gulf of Mexico.

The mineral wealth of Central and Southern Africa, the High Andes, Amazonia and Eastern Asia will also be significant sources of potential conflict. Two-thirds of the strategically important metal cobalt is mined in central Africa; China has a similar proportion of world reserves of tungsten; and rock phosphate reserves – essential constituents of artificial fertilizers – are concentrated in North Africa.

Against this, the continuing food grain surpluses of the US and the European Union (EU) will give them considerable leverage in their pursuit of foreign policy options, with the grain and corn belts of central US and Canada dominating world grain exports.

Migration

There is likely to be an upsurge in population movements, caused partly by a desire for a better lifestyle but also by environmental pressures. This is already leading to what has been called 'militant migration'. Pressure will become more intense on North America and Western Europe, the latter likely to experience much increased migratory pressures from North Africa, the Middle East and parts of Eastern Europe and the former Soviet Union. This is already producing an anti-immigration reaction in Western Europe, which is leading not just to the rise of far-right political parties, but to using tactics such as the fear of unemployment and other perceived consequences of immigration by centre-right and centrist parties in pursuit of electoral popularity.

Economic competition

Increased economic competition between three major trading groups, North America, the EU and Japan is also likely. The US is in relative economic decline yet has the only highly developed capability to project military force world-wide. It may have been happy to demonstrate this capability in the Gulf in 1991, with Germany and Japan paying part of the bill for protecting their access to Gulf oil, but there is no guarantee that the US will act in such a semi-surrogate role again. In practice, it is more likely to compete more forcefully with Europe and East Asia in the economic sphere and to use its military forces more specifically to support its own interests.

The Southern response

Finally, and most importantly, the developing North–South axis will lead to a more vigorous political and military response from the South. This is already shown in the evolving foreign policies of major states such as China and India, and the pursuit of advanced weapons capabilities by a number of states. It is complicated in other parts of the South by anti-elitism, militant nationalisms, regional separatism and a variety of religious fundamentalisms. Collectively this means that any idea that the control of human aspirations by northern economic interests and local southern elites through economic dominance, political control and direct or indirect repression is wishful thinking. It simply will not last.

People on the fringe of a reasonable life, particularly if they are educated to an awareness of the living standards of the North, will not tolerate the maintenance of a polarized world. These 'underclass responses' in the South are almost impossible to predict with any certainty as to their evolution, location or effects. They may express themselves in guerrilla campaigns of almost messianic fervour, as with the *Sendero Luminosa* phenomenon in Peru, with militant nationalism as in India, or religious fundamentalism as in North Africa and the Levant. When these movements directly affect northern interests, they may easily be seen by the military (and others) as a new type of 'threat' – altogether welcome as an alternative to the former Soviet Union. The tenor of the northern response to these possibilities is not encouraging. One recent US military study advocated strategies to target 'that swirling pot of poison made up of zealots, crazies, drug runners and terrorists'.[8]

MILITARY RESPONSES IN THE NORTH

The easing of Cold War tensions leaves a massive military complex searching for a new role. Protecting the interests of the wealthier North against any kind of threat from the South is an eminently saleable policy. It is one for which some military strategists have been preparing for many years. The search for a new enemy to replace the Soviet threat is both urgent and intense and that from the global ghettoes might be just too good to ignore! In the military literature and in rapidly changing defence postures of significant northern states, already there is a re-orientation of military perspectives towards a North–South axis.

From a military strategist's perspective, major threats to northern security might be expressed in two broad ways. One is instability, through movements which threaten the power of local elites and related northern interests, as has frequently happened in Latin America. The other is the evolution of regimes thought to pose a more open and direct threat, especially in areas of high resource significance, as with Iraq in 1990–91.

In either case, the prime response which we see developing, especially in the US, is a military response. This takes many forms and is common to most branches of the armed forces. For example, the US Navy and Marine Corps believe that their historic capacity to project military force by means of amphibious operations or use of carrier-based air power gives them an unrivalled capacity to 'keep the violent peace' in the South after the Cold War.

The US Air Force (USAF) is developing tactics to enable it to undertake extraordinarily long-range bombing strategies and to destroy specific kinds of targets such as deeply protected bunkers. The US Army, too, is bidding for extended funding for special operations forces designed to counter local threats to US interests or the status of pro-US governmental elites. Even the Strategic Defence Initiative (SDI or 'Star Wars') is now being adapted to take on Third World missiles. Revised nuclear strategies, and even new kinds of nuclear weapons, are being researched to allow a response to North–South tensions. I will return to these later.

The way these 'new threats' to world stability are represented varies from the crude through to the measured. An example of the former is seen in the Reed Report, a draft of which was leaked to the Washington press early in 1991. This *Strategic Deterrence Study* was undertaken for the US Strategic Air Command late in 1990, and paid particular attention to future Third World threats against US interests.[9] Its terms of reference state the belief that 'the growing wealth of petro-nations and newly hegemonic powers is available to bullies and crazies, if they gain control, to wreak havoc on world tranquillity'.

The study itself calls for a new nuclear targeting strategy which will include the ability to assemble 'a Nuclear Expeditionary Force... primarily for use against China or Third World targets', which is required because 'Nations with the wealth and ideological fervor to pursue nuclear programs, no matter what the time and cost, are very different' from traditional nuclear powers such as Britain and France. North Korea, Algeria, Libya, Iran, and of course Iraq fit this bill. To quote: 'They and their terrorist cousins are more likely driven by...the desire to...terrorise, blackmail, coerce, or destroy' among other motives.

A more thoughtful American assessment of the evolving security outlook was given by Roger Barnett, writing in the *Proceedings of the US Naval Institute* in mid-1992. The *Proceedings* has been one of the most interesting journals in reflecting new military postures, not least because of the long-term navy and marine corps concern with power projection.[10]

Barnett argues for enhancing military forces for regional intervention, and includes in his future security threats the problems associated with the break-up of the Warsaw Pact. He goes on to look at a range of developing problems, including in his list of primary threats to western security:

- widening economic differentials between the economic North and South;
- impact of high-technology weapons and weapons of mass destruction on the ability – and thus the willingness – of the weak to take up arms against the strong;
- inequitable distribution of world food supplies, and the dislocation of millions of people because of famine, wars and natural disasters;
- use of force or of terrorism to attempt to redress grievances or resolve problems.

Barnett's analysis is impressive because it attempts to rise above the crude rhetoric of 'bullies and crazies' and gives some indication of the background forces being seen to operate.

For the most part, however, military postures and tactics operate at a more basic level. By now examining military trends in detail, particularly in the US, we can see how military forces and activities are actually being reshaped and the kind of threats this implies. The US is the lead state in such developments although similar, smaller scale examples can be seen in other western states.

The US nuclear response

By the early 1980s, the US and the Soviet Union were in the middle of an intense build-up of nuclear forces. This was curbed later in the decade, and the Intermediate-Range Nuclear Forces (INF) and Strategic Arms Reductions Talks (START) agreements heralded some impressive declines in armaments. Fears of a surge in nuclear proliferation proved excessive, as Argentina and Brazil curbed their nuclear ambitions and the rate of proliferation in Asia and the Middle East seemed to slow.

By the early 1990s, US perceptions of proliferation changed for several reasons. After the Gulf War of 1991, it became clear that Iraq was far further down the road towards nuclear status than had been realized. Pakistan appeared on the brink of nuclear status, estimates of North Korea's nuclear potential were raised and the Soviet Union had split into numerous republics, four of which had nuclear weapons. There was also a surge of interest in the spread of ballistic missiles, especially Scud derivatives and Chinese systems, and a recognition that many states still saw chemical weapons as a cheap alternative to nuclear arms.

The US believed that a number of states antagonistic to its interests wanted specifically to develop weapons of mass destruction. There was also a suspicion that the treatment of Iraq, with its status changing from trusted ally to deepest enemy in the space of three months, would encourage such states to acquire a means of deterrence against possible future US action. By 1992, the official US line was that its own nuclear weapons programmes had been curtailed, but there were repeated indications that new systems were being designed, specifically for Third World contingencies. The Reed Report's proposals were reportedly being backed up by the planning of new weapons, including electromagnetic pulse (EMP) bombs for disabling electronic systems, small nuclear warheads for destroying missiles armed with biological warheads and earth-penetrating warheads for destroying bunkers which were too well protected for conventional bombs to destroy.[11]

While official confirmation of these trends is, unsurprisingly, hard to find, the proportion of the defence budget accounted for by 'black' (secret) programmes will rise in 1994. The military literature has also been full of articles pointing to the threat of a proliferated world, some suggesting tough measures to pre-empt such a situation. Republican

Congressman John Kyle, a member of the House Armed Services Committee, expressed a widely-held view of the dangers, citing the following threats to US interests:

- US intelligence officials say some two dozen countries may possess or may be developing weapons of mass destruction and the means to deliver them.
- At least 25 countries are pursuing chemical weapon programs and many of these have biological programs as well.
- 15 or so countries have operational ballistic missiles, with more scheduled to join the ranks in the coming decade.[12]

Kyle advocated strengthening intelligence-gathering as a priority, along with greater cooperation with allies, and more emphasis on the development, with Russia, of the planned Global Protection System. This is a 'son-of-Star-Wars' derivative of SDI aimed specifically at Third World missile threats. He said, however, that this was in all probability not sufficient to control trends in proliferation, and advocated a willingness to take military action against potential nuclear states and their sources of supply.

The US response to missile proliferation

If an increasing source of concern to the US military is the long-term spread of nuclear weapons, then worries over missile proliferation are much more immediate and permeate much of the military. For them, their experience in the Gulf War is salutary. The Iraqi Scud missiles were of little military significance, but they had a great political and psychological importance, especially with respect to the attacks on Israel. The USAF was tied down for more than two weeks trying to find the Scud launchers. Although publicly it spoke of great successes in the 'Scud hunt', post-war assessments suggested that very few launchers or missiles were destroyed on the ground, and even the Patriot defences were of limited value, tending mainly to fragment the incoming Scuds as they neared their targets, turning them into clusters of high velocity shrapnel.

In the past two years, the lessons of the Scud hunts have had an effect on the US and many Third World states. The US is seeking to build a political and military defence against missiles, while other states, seeing their political value, try to buy or develop them. According to one Washington defence newsletter published in May 1993, countries which have sought to acquire missiles include Afghanistan, Algeria, Argentina, Brazil, China, Egypt, India, Indonesia, Iran, Iraq, Israel, Libya, North Korea, Pakistan, Saudi Arabia, South Africa, Taiwan, Vietnam and Yemen.[13]

One US response has been to seek to develop the Global Protection System, which was an outcome of the June 1992 Summit between Presidents Bush and Yeltsin: 'The two leaders announced the ambitious plan to implement a global system that enables both countries and their allies to share early warning data, work to curb ballistic missile proliferation and seek avenues of technology cooperation...'[14] This cooperation will include a sharing of ballistic missile defence technology which formed part of the SDI programme and its Soviet equivalent. Ironically, these two technological programmes were formerly in intense competition and now will, together, provide protection from new enemies in the South.

SDI itself was directed primarily at countering attacks by intercontinental range ballistic missiles and was criticized as a hugely wasteful, probably unworkable, programme. The 'lower end' of SDI was concerned with the threat from slower missiles of medium and intermediate range, where anti-missile systems could be effective, and this is now getting the funding; the rest was consigned to the scrap-heap by the incoming Clinton administration.

The first product will be the Theatre High Altitude Area Defence missile (THAAD) developed by Lockheed which in mid-1992 received a 4-year $689 million contract to complete it.[15] Lockheed hopes to win a further $4 billion worth of contracts for their air-transportable missile system, which should be able to intercept missiles with a range of up to 1800 miles (about twice that of improved Scuds). THAAD is a system for the US Army, but the US Navy is advocating its Aegis missile control system for theatre missile defence. It claims that most areas of security concern to the US could be protected by anti-aircraft cruisers deployed in neighbouring seas.

However fast the US and its allies develop programmes to counter one threat, new threats are seen to arise. As one official noted: 'What the US Tomahawks did to the Iraqis during the Persian Gulf War was not lost on our adversaries...'.[16] The most recent is with low-flying cruise missiles developed in the South. A Pentagon report in early 1993 claimed that several countries, including China, Syria and Iran, would have stealthy cruise missiles with chemical and biological warheads between the years 2000 and 2010.[17] Some Pentagon officials therefore claimed that the SDI Office was concentrating too much on the threat of ballistic missile proliferation, whereas cruise missiles would become more significant.

In response to this trend, the USAF and US Navy were reported to be working on a joint programme to tackle cruise missiles:

> The plan owes some of its technological roots to the Defense Department's Air Defense Initiative (ADI). The plan links US ground and air-based sensors, Air Force and Navy interceptor aircraft, rapid data transfer and specially modified air-to-air missiles into a high-tech net to snag cruise missiles. It differs from early ADI plans in that it protects allied troops far from continental US defenses. Because many of its elements are airborne, the system can deploy with expeditionary forces into a regional hotspot.[18]

These adaptations to the post-Cold War world are for programmes concerned with the risk of all-out conflict. The changes in military strategy go far beyond this, however. They extend to a huge range of conventional forces, many of them involving rapid and fundamental changes in outlook, but all concerned with meeting a perceived challenge of many different kinds of threats coming not from one single enemy but from many – the 'jungle full of snakes' as the CIA director put it so precisely.

US air power anywhere

Although President Carter cancelled the USAF's new B-1 strategic bomber in 1977, President Reagan re-activated the programme four years later. The B-1B, as it was now called, was to be a nuclear-armed, low-level strategic bomber – a core part of the Reagan military expansion of the 1980s for use in East–West conflict.

An important parallel programme to the new bomber was the development of the nuclear-armed air-launched cruise missile (ALCM), first deployed in 1982, both for the new B-1B and many older B-52s. The new stand-off ALCM could be launched up to 1500 miles away from the target. By 1986, some 1700 ALCMs had been produced before the programme was curtailed in favour of the more sophisticated advanced cruise missile.[19]

As the Cold War tensions ebbed away, a decision was taken towards the end of the 1980s to modify part of the ALCM fleet by removing the nuclear warheads and replacing them with conventional high-explosive warheads. This was a 'black' programme and remained highly classified throughout its early development. On the first night of the Gulf War in

January 1991 a number of these ALCMs formed part of the longest air raid in history. A flight of B-52 bombers took off from Louisiana and, supported by multiple air-to-air refuellings, made a non-stop 14,000-mile round-trip flight to within a few hundred miles of the Iraqi border, where they launched ALCMs at targets within Iraq. This operation, which remained secret until several months after the Gulf War, was used to prove that the USAF could use its long-range bombers to attack almost any point on the earth's surface from bases in the US. It was a demonstration of a developing USAF doctrine: that its bombers constituted the fastest and most versatile way of projecting US military force abroad.

Since then, a large part of the USAF strategic inventory has been re-configured for the new world order, so the USAF can strike with conventional and nuclear weapons against targets threatening US security. Some hundreds of ALCMs have had their nuclear warheads removed, many replaced with high-explosive warheads but some with EMP which can disable a wide range of electronic devices.[20] They are also being coated in radar-absorbing material giving them 'semi-stealth' characteristics to make detection and destruction more difficult.

By the early 1990s, the 100 B-1Bs produced during the 1980s were scheduled to be re-fitted to take conventional weapons. This changeover is proceeding slowly and with some opposition on grounds of cost. There are now plans to make the even more expensive B-2 'stealth' bomber a platform primarily for conventional weapons. The USAF will then maintain a mixed fleet of B-52, B-1B and B-2 bombers, all capable of very long-range strike missions, a plan dubbed the 'bomber road map' during 1992. The B-2 is currently being produced in very low numbers, but its stealthy characteristics mean that it can overfly the air space of potential opponents in the South with very little risk to the aircrew. This is a key factor in current US military posture where the risk of captured military becoming high-profile prisoners is regarded as unacceptable.

The USAF wants to maintain a strategic force of 184 operational aircraft, and its 'bomber road map' strategy calls for the ability to hit 750 separate targets within the first five days of a war conducted at a distance from the USA.[21] The B-2 can already carry 16 precision-guided bombs per flight and there are plans to develop a very accurate 2000lb bomb which could be used specifically to hit mobile targets such as missile launchers.

The USAF is also developing a number of programmes for its tactical bombers, also intended for use primarily in relatively small regional conflicts. Because of the concern about medium-range ballistic missiles such as advanced Scud derivatives, considerable development is going into combinations of intelligence-gathering and weapons systems which can destroy such missiles on their mobile launchers. The failure to find most Iraqi Scud launchers during the Gulf War has prompted two programmes, *Precision Strike Demonstration* and *Talon Sword*, both of which coordinate battlefield sensors, command centres and attack aircraft.[22]

A related problem has been the sale of advanced surface-to-air missiles to Southern states by the former Soviet Union. These missiles cannot be jammed by current USAF jamming aircraft such as the EF-111A.[23] A budget of $250 million has so far been allocated to a System Improvement Programme to upgrade the EF-111 and the US Navy's EA6B jamming aircraft so they can counter these missiles.

In essence, then, the USAF now sees its role very much as power projection, either using long-range heavy bombers or tactical forces for forward deployment to meet regional threats. This change has been aided by the merging in June 1992 of the USAF's Tactical Air Command and most of the Strategic Air Command to create a new Air Combat Command, which can combine strategic and tactical forces in pursuit of global reach. An example of this approach was seen early in 1993:

> The Air Force did something unusual with its B-1s last March. It sent a pair of the bombers from Ellsworth AFB, South Dakota, via Guam, to the Republic of Korea, where they set down on an American air base within easy striking distance of a hostile neighbouring nation.
>
> The faraway, in-your-face deployment of the B-1s was part of exercise *Team Spirit*, a muscular US/ROK combined-arms military exercise involving airforce units from Pacific Air Force (PACAF) and Air Combat Command (ACC). Among other things, it demonstrated to North Korea, now likely a nuclear threat, just how diverse and deadly US air power has become.
>
> By using B-1s in the exercise, including a third bomber out of Guam, the Air Force underlined a message delivered with a bang in the Persian Gulf War – that bombers armed with non-nuclear bombs and based in the continental United States are now big guns in US global power.[24]

This role for the USAF was highlighted in a recent Rand Corporation study:

> In future major regional conflicts, national political and military leaders are likely to place a premium on US forces that can deploy rapidly over

long distances, swiftly destroy invading armoured forces as well as fixed assets, and engage the enemy effectively while placing minimal numbers of American service personnel in harm's way.

A quantitative analysis taking these factors into consideration shows that landbased air forces – heavy bombers and fighter-bombers – are likely to provide the lion's share of US power projection capability in future conflicts, at least in the critical days or weeks of the war.

The analysis shows that US heavy bombers, with long range and large payloads of offensive weapons, have the potential to project conventional firepower rapidly and effectively, providing critical capabilities early in a 'short-warning' conflict. In the opening days of such a war, bombers are uniquely capable of delivering heavy firepower against fixed targets and, in the case of the stealthy B-2, invading armies.[25]

The USAF has adapted rapidly to the collapse of the old enemy and is now geared up to intervene rapidly and with great force wherever US interests may be threatened.

US sea power

The changed air force orientation is, inevitably, a doctrine which clashes directly with the US Navy and Marine Corps. These two branches of the US armed forces have traditionally considered themselves to be the real exponents of power projection. The marines' historic role, outside of major war, had been to implement foreign policy in numerous small interventions, especially in Latin America.[26] The navy had a more clear-cut strategic role with its long-range missile submarines and also played a central role in containing Soviet naval forces. Much of its strategy was thus concerned with open ocean or 'blue water' naval warfare, but it also saw itself as having an important secondary role in protecting US interests throughout the world. Many navy bases in Asia and the Pacific had twin roles; a primary function of contributing to a possible war effort against the Eastern bloc, and a secondary role of constraining Soviet adventurism abroad and any non-Soviet threat.

The US capacity for military force projection was concentrated especially on the Middle East and South West Asia. The increasing strategic importance of Persian Gulf oil reserves had been recognized after the oil price rises of 1973/4 and 1979/80. President Carter had called for an increase in the US capability to project military force in his 1977 Presidential Directive 11, which led up to the creation of the Joint Rapid Deployment Task Force (Rapid Deployment Force or RDF) in 1980.

By the early 1980s, the US already had the world's largest military capacity for projecting force, much of it naval. By the middle of the decade this included 14 operational aircraft carriers, each of which could be deployed at the centre of a carrier battle group with escorts of cruisers, destroyers, frigates, submarines and supply ships. This gave the US Navy carrier-based air power some five times larger than all other navies of the world combined. A further expansion of naval power was undertaken in the early 1980s with the re-activation of four World War II battleships, but armed with Tomahawk sea-launched cruise missiles. At the same time, the US Marine Corps, numbering around 190,000 personnel, was substantially re-equipped.

An additional development was the enhancement of logistic support with heavy investment in container ships (capable, for example, of transporting the equipment for a complete armoured division to the Persian Gulf) and improving the techniques of pre-positioning supplies by ship to a crisis area to support troops. Unless army or marine forces are fully supplied with food, fuel, munitions and other stores, their capabilities in combat decline rapidly. US military strategy under the Reagan build-up called for the capacity to act with force virtually anywhere in the world. While not widely recognized, this revolution in logistic support was probably more significant in terms of increased force projection capabilities than the expansion of the carrier battle groups or the re-activation of battleships.

The developing logistic policy of the 1980s was tailored largely, though not entirely, to South West Asia, including the Middle East. The British-owned island of Diego Garcia in the Indian Ocean was an essential component of this strategy and was leased to the US. This gave the US the capability to intervene in the Middle East which was notably absent during the oil crisis of the early 1970s.

Finally, and specifically relevant to the Persian Gulf, the RDF was elevated to the status of an entirely new unified military command to be known as US Central Command (CENTCOM). Just as Pacific Command was responsible for US security interests in the Pacific, and Southern Command for Latin America, so CENTCOM had a particular zone of responsibility – North-East Africa and South-West Asia; 19 countries stretching in an arc from Kenya through the Middle East to Pakistan.

By late 1984, the forces available to CENTCOM included four army divisions and one brigade, together with a marine division and a brigade, backed up with comprehensive air and sea support. A key concept was rapid deployment: a complete army brigade of over 4000 troops with comprehensive air-mobile artillery and air defences was available for air transport at 20 hours notice. By the late 1980s, CENTCOM had been further expanded and had some 300,000 personnel from all four services assigned to it. While most of the forces and the HQ of CENTCOM were located in the US, the forces were trained and equipped for rapid movement to, and deployment in, the Middle East and surrounding areas.

Keeping the violent peace

The expansion of the navy's power projection capabilities in the early 1980s may have been primarily to execute the new maritime strategy against the Soviet Union, but it led to a world-wide enhancement of military readiness. As Admiral James Watkins remarked in 1986:

> We now maintain a continual presence in the Indian Ocean, Persian Gulf and Caribbean, as well as our more traditional forward deployments to the Mediterranean and Western Pacific. Although we are not at war today, our operating tempo has been about 20 percent higher than during the Vietnam War.[27]

This military readiness was christened 'keeping the violent peace' in the Third World, and naval forces such as aircraft carrier battle groups and amphibious warfare ships were essential for such a strategy. According to two US Navy Commanders, Robinson and Benkert, it differed from the requirements for global war with the Soviet Union in three broad ways. First, a wartime strategy, in their view, concentrates on countering overt Soviet aggression while, 'peacetime strategy objectives are more diffuse and perhaps best characterized as furthering an ill-defined set of interests of which countering the Soviets is only part, although a very important part.' Second, a violent peace strategy is inherently less structured and clear-cut in its objectives and processes. Finally, political and diplomatic considerations may dominate or circumscribe military considerations, at least in the early stages of a crisis. The major aims of a violent peace strategy are:

- protecting sea lines of communication and transit rights;
- allowing the US continued access to resources and markets; and
- demonstrating US interests overseas.

The US Navy is now well placed to respond to perceived threats from the South. By the early 1990s, and after the experience of the Gulf War, the navy began to reconfigure its forces away from the Soviet threat and towards the Third World. As most of the navy had been directed towards the East–West conflict, it could easily stand some cuts while retaining a very high level of power projection potential. The main thrust of the new strategy was a heavy concentration on coastal warfare, land attack and support of amphibious forces.

A Navy/Marine Corps White Paper '...From the Sea', signed on 29 September 1992, commenced:

> The world has changed dramatically in the last two years, and America's national security policy has also changed. As a result, the priorities of the Navy and Marine Corps have shifted, leading to this broad assessment of the future direction of our maritime forces.[28]

The nature of this new direction is that:

> Our strategy has shifted from a focus on a global threat to a focus on regional challenges and opportunities. While the prospect of global war has receded, we are entering a period of enormous uncertainty in regions critical to our national interests. Our forces can help to shape the future in ways favourable to our interests by underpinning our alliances, precluding threats, and helping to preserve the strategic position we won at the end of the Cold War.[29]

An indication of where the threats might arise comes in a report of a recent wargaming exercise at the Marine Corps Combat Development Command at Quantico, where scenarios involving Cuba, Libya, North Korea and Iraq were played out.[30] The emphasis was on rapid and surprise landings from over the horizon, using new generations of fast landing craft including air cushion vehicles. The marines, too, now see a bright new future for the Corps. As their commander, General Carl Mundy, put it recently:

> The era of the Marines has returned. If you look back to the 1920s and 1930s, Marines came to be known as 'State Department troops'. The reason for that description was that many people thought the despatching of the Marines to foreign lands did not connote an act of war but was simply a representation of US interests abroad.[31]

Although in recent years the marines have operated almost entirely from their own assault ships and have maintained their own air force, they are now cooperating much more closely with the navy. For example early in

1993, a Marine Air-Ground Task Force of 600 personnel and 10 helicopters was deployed on board the aircraft carrier *USS Theodore Roosevelt*. The carrier left behind some of its anti-submarine warfare aircraft, but still maintained almost all its force of fighters and strike aircraft. This combination gave it the capability for a much wider range of activities than in the Cold War years, including operations in low intensity conflicts such as counter-insurgency operations in support of friendly government elites.[32]

At a more general level, naval analysts argue forcefully that the navy is the best equipped force for power projection, pointing to its highly mobile aircraft carriers and its substantial cruise missile force. There is continuing competition between the navy and the air force. The USAF argues that strategic bombers can hit almost anywhere in the world from the US, and the navy argues that the versatility of carrier-based aircraft is superior.[33]

The US Army

The army is not to be left out of this debate. It is arguing that it too has a system suitable for deep strike against targets in regional conflicts – the Army Tactical Missile System (ATACMS), while the air force promotes precision-guided bombs and the navy, sea-launched cruise missiles:

> US Air Force control over precision strike missions could erode rapidly with the advent of US Army and Navy deep-strike systems that can smash enemy targets faster and more decisively than air-launched weaponry, US military and civilian sources say.
>
> The role each service should play in the increasingly critical deep-strike mission is a subject of contentious debate within the Joint Chiefs of Staff. Pentagon sources say most regional commanders argue the Army should place an increased role in deep strikes...
>
> Loren Larsen, Deputy Director of the Pentagon's deepstrike systems office said Nov. 9 that the Army's emphasis on rapid communications and the fast-flying ground-launched Army Tactical Missile System (ATACMS) gives the service 'a significant leg-up' over the Air Force, which relies on piloted aircraft that react more slowly. The ATACMS can be used to destroy a target at long range within 10 minutes of its detection while Air Force pilots are still en route, he said. Navy use of the Tomahawk cruise missile and potential use of a ship-launched version of the ATACMS also rival Air Force capabilities, he said.[34]

We see here, as so often during the Cold War, rivalry between the armed forces as each seeks the biggest budgets for policing the new world order and protecting US interests. While the air force and navy (and the 'son of Star Wars') seem the obvious candidates for new spending, the army has been doing its best to argue its case, even as troops are being withdrawn from Europe. Use of ATACMS in regional conflicts is one of the few systems available to the army at a time when the navy and air force are making the running in military policy transition. In one other area, the army is pushing hard to maintain its position – special operations forces.

As with the marine corps, army special operations forces act principally in low intensity conflicts. They expect to increase their spheres of operations in an era of diverse conflicts and security interests in the South. They act with units of the other services in US Special Operations Command, and there is a major re-equipment programme under way:

> The US Special Operations Command (USSOCOM) identified a broad spectrum of technology thrusts in its new posture statement. To cope with the rapid proliferation of military technologies in Third World countries, special operations forces (SOF) will require new equipment and personal gear that can provide a defense against current sensors.[35]

Programmes include a series of major upgradings to support aircraft and helicopters, new long-range support craft with an open-ocean range of over 1000 miles, and the provision of newly modified submarines for secret delivery of forces into hostile areas.[36] The army's role in policing the new world order may be smaller than that of the other services, but it is determined to take its place within the new strategy.

Areas of action

While small-scale intervention by the US may occur wherever local interests appear threatened, three areas of action are pre-eminent. The Persian Gulf region, with two-thirds of the world's proven oil reserves, is considered of fundamental importance to the US, especially as its own oil reserves are depleted and it becomes a major oil importer. Secondly, any threats to US economic and political interests in Latin America are regarded as particularly significant and in need of control. Finally, there is an increasing likelihood of a resort to military force to control the proliferation of weapons of mass destruction.

Parallel processes in Europe

The US has by far the most powerful military forces in the world. But the re-orientation of forces and postures in which it is currently engaged are mirrored among its allies. Though NATO as a whole is still primarily oriented towards the security of Europe, the development of its Rapid Reaction Corps and its increased emphasis on the extended deployment of air power show elements of the US trends.

Individual NATO states give clearer indications of an outlook which parallels that of the US. An example is France's continuing commitment to carrier-based naval air power and rapid reaction army and air force units. Britain is particularly interesting: there are modest cuts in the defence budget under way, but coupled with a marked and quite costly re-ordering of posture. The defence cuts in Britain have fallen most heavily on those units in the forces which have been concerned specifically with the East—West confrontation, including a proportionally large cut-back in ground forces, especially armoured units in Germany, substantial cuts in naval anti-submarine forces and cuts in deep strike aircraft. While some tactical nuclear systems have been withdrawn, the Trident strategic nuclear force, still under development, appears to be in transition to give it an added 'sub-strategic capability', probably including a relatively small-yield nuclear warhead. The air force has lost some Tornado bomber squadrons but will retain almost all of its transport capability, including tanker aircraft. The Royal Marines suffer little in the way of cuts. The most interesting development is the changing make-up of the Royal Navy, with the withdrawal of a significant proportion of escorts as well as all four new conventionally-powered submarines. At the same time, the three small aircraft-carriers will all be maintained in service, a helicopter carrier has recently been ordered and it is likely that the two ageing assault ships will be replaced. Thus, Cold War defences are cut back, but military forces of use in small and medium-scale power projection are maintained. Together with Trident, these enable Britain to maintain some of its pretensions to global reach in an uncertain world. It is part of the same process, as in the US, preparing for 'a crowded, glowering planet'.

Even more intriguing are the developing links with the armed forces of the former Soviet bloc. Russia's concern with instability on its southern borders already extends to seeking links with the US in ballistic missile defence. The idea of a Global Protection System discussed by Presidents Bush and Yeltsin in 1992 is not 'global' at all but much more a shielding of the North from a potential missile threat from the South.

PEACEFUL ALTERNATIVES

Curbing the development of a North–South axis of confrontation is intellectually and politically difficult. It requires a reversal of the main threads of northern strategic ethnocentrism which has seen all world problems in terms of its own interests – previously East–West, now North–South. The northern strategists and politicians will readily view threats to a new world order as being legitimate security concerns which should best be met by modifying military strategies to meet such threats. This is a particularly seductive viewpoint at a time of defence budget cuts.

In reality, the complex of global security problems now developing is not best approached from a military standpoint, indeed this is almost certain to be thoroughly counterproductive. Solutions lie principally in the political and economic arenas.

The core problems of poverty, environmental constraint and militarization require five responses:

1. Processes of militarization have to be reversed.
2. Northern industrialized countries have radically to change their policies towards the South.
3. Development policies encouraged by such change must be in a form which will ensure accelerated yet environmentally sustainable development.
4. Future development in the industrialized countries must itself be sustainable, recognizing that the major global environmental problems are caused primarily by the activities of these countries.
5. There must be a change in international behaviour to ensure a rapid and effective response to any future changes in the global ecosystem.

This requires a process of political evolution that is based on the concept of common human security and on a willingness to extend greatly the timescales of political action. In an environmentally constrained planet, there is no alternative to seeing security as synonymous with peace and justice – self-centred security is no longer tenable. This idea is only just beginning to emerge through the work of the Palme, Brundtland and South Commissions.

To counter militarization requires an agenda for arms control and disarmament which would amount to a rapid reversal of the patterns of the past 40 years. While the ending of the Cold War will certainly see significant cuts in that spending, our concern must be global militarization. The agenda has, therefore, to extend to addressing those threats which, while usually originating in the context of the Cold War, also carry global risks. They include the full range of weapons of mass destruction, whether nuclear, chemical, biological or conventional, together with control of arms transfers and the progressive demilitarization of military manufacture.

The processes of demilitarization and arms industry conversion are complex and incur costs, yet cutting of as much as one half of global military spending over the next decade would release resources hugely in excess of anything previously committed to development assistance and environmental repair.

Of the other four areas for action, the first and foremost is the re-ordering of North–South relations. This requires comprehensive trade, debt and aid reform. Trade reform entails commodity agreements providing for progressively higher and stable primary commodity earnings for the South. Tariff preferences and commodity processing incentives are essential to encourage substantially higher export earnings, giving greater potential for investment in internal development. Debt cancellation rather than debt re-scheduling is needed to counter the debt crisis, and development assistance should be in grant rather than loan form and aimed principally at basic needs. These necessary changes in North–South development relationships are both radical and fundamental. They represent a near-total re-ordering of attitudes which would, over a period of years, involve a redistribution of wealth from North to South. This is a reversal of the pattern of the last several decades.

While the changes above involve a basic shift in the approach to international development, they do not of themselves address the issue of environmental constraints. The need in both the South and North is for patterns of development which are, to the best of our knowledge of environmental processes, sustainable in the long term. Conditions for sustainable development aim to prevent local, regional and especially global environmental deterioration.[37] Renewable resources, whether crops, forests or fisheries, must be maintained in a manner which ensures their continued productivity. Over-exploited ecosystems which have already deteriorated must be returned to a state in which sustainable exploitation is possible. More generally, any exploited ecosystem must contribute a broadly similar level of energy flows and materials recycling to the natural ecosystem it replaces; and substantial areas of natural ecosystem must be preserved to maintain species diversity.

Any depletion of non-renewable resources must involve depletion only to a defined minimal stock. Any further exploitation would require newly discovered reserves. Part of the earnings from the exploitation of non-renewable resources should be invested in more efficient use of these resources (recycling, avoidance of wastage) or their replacement with renewable resources. While zero emission of pollutants into the biosphere may rarely be possible, emissions must not exceed recognized limits (whether local, regional or global).

It follows that a greatly improved standard of living for the majority of the world's population must be achieved using patterns of development greatly different from those pursued by the industrialized North. The massive and ecologically inefficient over-use of resources by the North must also be curbed.

North–South economic relations could be transformed in a manner which simultaneously redresses North–South inequalities and allows for environmentally sustainable resource use. For example, a commodity agreement covering a major non-renewable resource could involve a progressive increase in price, which would encourage conservation in consumption and allow an increased potential for sustainable economic and social development in the areas of production. This will not happen unless policies are constructed which encourage it to happen.

Switching away from conventional military approaches to security to such changed environment and development policies faces three core forms of opposition. First, there is the problem of political and economic timescales. Political systems tend to support planning which shows a social or economic return on political investment within five to ten years at the most. One to two years is often preferable, or even weeks or months prior to an election! Similarly, economic returns are normally sought within much less than ten years. Political and economic planning to counter environmental degradation may show little positive return in one or even two decades. To implement sustainable development which also addresses North–South polarization will involve a degree of planning and co-ordination that is antagonistic to the broadly free market approach which has dominated much of western politics in the 1980s. Secondly, the longer term effects of major environmental trends are difficult to predict with any kind of certainty. It is therefore easy to adopt best-case scenarios in order to avoid facing up to uncomfortable choices. Finally, and most intractable, evolving a sustainable and peaceful global economic system inevitably means considerable costs for the wealthy industrialized states of the North, especially the Group of Seven – the US, Canada, Britain, France, Germany, Italy and Japan.

Common global security implies radical cuts in resource use by the North, together with the transition to stable economies and a costly commitment to sustainable development in the South. This will be in direct opposition to those schools of thought which believe that existing levels of wealth and consumption can be maintained in the North, and that the countries of the North have a legitimate international right to maintain their standards and styles of living, if need be by military force.

2

Conflict and Development: What Kinds of Policies can Reduce the Damaging Impact of War?

Frances Stewart and Ken Wilson

Wars, especially civil wars, have been visibly one of the most potent causes of human suffering and underdevelopment in the South. Around 15 million deaths were caused (directly or indirectly) by war in developing countries between 1950 and 1990, the vast majority of whom were civilians. In 12 of the 16 countries with the highest mortality rates from war between 1970 and 1990 more than two-thirds were civilian deaths. Most of the countries with the worst economic and social indicators have experienced civil or international wars. Examples abound of conflict precipitating catastrophic declines in the economy and the general well-being of populations. Yet much social and economic comparative analysis ignores countries at war. It is high time that this changed. Measures are needed both to reduce the level of conflict in the South, and to enable countries to weather better the economic effects of conflict.

In this chapter, we examine the links between conflict and development. First, we explore the different types of conflict and their roots. Next, we examine the impacts of conflict upon economic development and how far economic policy can limit the degree to which conflict is damaging. Third, we suggest a synthesis which shows the varying ways in which the state capacity and will to act developmentally can limit the damage caused by war and can speed recovery. Finally, we illustrate these themes with a case study of Mozambique.

ECONOMIC DEVELOPMENT AND THE ROOTS OF CONFLICT

It is extremely difficult to generalize about the causes of military conflict in the South as each war has its own multiplicity of causes. While clearly the displacement of Cold War rivalry into the Third World made conflict much more likely, prolonged and damaging, internal factors also produced conflict. Indeed it is possible to see a complex interplay between the two. The involvement of superpowers tended both to exacerbate poor economic and public policy, thus further reducing state legitimacy, and to increase the level of armament.

We found we could identify five general scenarios for Third World military conflict to help in the analysis of the costs of war. In all but those of an international nature, the relationship between state economic development policies and the start of conflict is central. These scenarios are important because they illustrate the nature of the economic impacts of war, the kinds of policies that are pursued and their effects.

1. International conflict between discrete states: Except for (often short-lived) border disputes these have tended to be relatively uncommon in the Third World. The most devastating in recent times has been the Iran-Iraq war.
2. Foreign invasion: This is a second international category though usually linked to local collaborators. It meets sustained local resistance. Examples include Vietnam, Heng Samrin's Cambodia, Afghanistan and Lebanon during the Israeli invasion. (Since nearly all civil wars involve military and political support from outsiders for the various factions there is sometimes an arbitrary line between international and national conflict.)
3. Civil war: Where a failure in state political and social integration leads to a violent struggle over the control of national resources and state revenues. Such conflict is particularly likely where windfall revenues can be earned from oil, mineral resources, or other off-shore resources, and/or where there are deeply established class, regional or ethnic disparities in wealth. One type of such conflict involves national liberation struggles (eg in the formerly white ruled states of Southern Africa, and perhaps in parts of Ethiopia-Eritrea), or broad-based guerrilla movements (eg El Salvador and Guatamala). A second type occurs where rebels

and state forces both draw upon popular but different constituencies. The state becomes the centre of bitter struggles for control and patronage. Wars of succession or of regionally-based struggles for state power then become established. The Biafran war, Sudan's two civil wars, pre-Museveni Uganda, the Kurdish conflicts, elements of Lebanon, and the new war in Angola fit into this type.

4. Destabilization of revolutionary states: States that pursue state socialist programmes become subject to military destabilization by regional or international superpowers. After an initial period of spirited resistance, destabilization saps the state's economic strength through diversion of resources into the military and through destruction of infrastructure. The state itself further undermines its capacity through over-ambitious planning. The resultant economic failures, which may be combined with a coercive modernizing approach, with power monopolized by a narrow cultural elite, fuel the erosion of state legitimacy. The post-independence Angolan and Mozambican wars fit this type, as does Sandinista Nicaragua.

5. Militarized disintegration: Wars caused by the collapse of state machinery, which may happen as a result of other kinds of war or political contests. This collapse usually combines a government's loss of legitimacy, its means of military domination, and a general politico-economic disintegration. It generates what is often referred to as 'war lord' politics, where new kinds of military-economic leaders expand into the economic and political vacuums generated by the disintegrating state. Such movements often originate in frontier wastelands and advance and may eventually overrun major economic and political centres. These political operators cleave countries apart, they engage in heavy looting and taxation of their areas, as well as the export of minerals, timber, drugs, ivory and other products. Liberia and Somalia are the archetypal examples, but in recent years the trend has been seen elsewhere, such as the Sudan and Afghanistan, the Thai-Cambodia border, Zaire, also, in some ways, in Chad and at certain points in Uganda. Echoes of such developments are seen in the drug wars and forest frontier societies of Central and South America.

Most wars contain – at different times and places – most elements of these different scenarios. For example, Afghanistan includes all but the first, and its causes and nature are not usefully reduced to a single interpretation. However, national economic processes are central, and in particular how the state's role in the economy is viewed by the population. Internal military conflicts tend to become serious where the state is too weak to maintain either its monopoly on the use of force or to sustain a common national economy and service structure. Conversely, military conflict can arise where the state becomes such a central actor in the distribution of resources that political accountability is lost, especially where it lacks the military power or coherence to suppress the resultant opposition. Popular guerrilla movements will then either resist state domination and/or seek to capture state resources for themselves. However, the importance of international support for opposition groups must not be forgotten, as for example in Southern Africa. It is this international context, as much as internal developments, that explains why so many countries in Africa are on the brink of wars of national disintegration.

THE IMPACTS OF WAR ON ECONOMIC DEVELOPMENT

The costs of war extend far beyond the physical casualties. Even in terms of mortality, the number of 'indirect' deaths has always been far higher than the direct deaths (except in the Iraq-Iran war). These deaths reflect principally the effects of destitution and famine precipitated by conflict and the damage to health and other service infrastructures.

The economic consequences of war are multiple and complex. Wars not only impose 'costs', but also lead to the transformation of state economic and political instruments and capacities. In fact, despite all their miseries, wars have often served in the longer term to restructure and modernize economies, at least in countries wealthy enough to weather the crises. However, the costs can be notionally divided into the immediate human costs and the longer term development costs. The division is artificial because the human costs (eg worsened nutrition and education) constitute developmental costs, while the developmental costs (eg destroyed infrastructure, negative growth) are among the causes of human suffering. Trying to be clear about these costs and who bears them is important if we are to find ways of avoiding or ameliorating them.

Human costs

We can analyse the human costs of war at three levels:

1. the *macro* or overall level of the economy and its outputs and incomes;
2. the *meso* level of specific policies and sectors, which determines how effects are distributed between sectors and groups; and
3. the *micro* or household level which is where individuals are affected.

Of course, the different levels interact with each other. We differentiate between effects of macro-level changes in the aggregate supply of goods and services, and their effects on individual entitlements to these, especially for vulnerable groups. There are two kinds of entitlements. Amartya Sen defined entitlements as the real command over resources, either from direct production, eg of food, or earnings and other sources of income which give people purchasing power over the commodities they need. In addition to these 'market' entitlements, we also focus on a second type, 'public entitlements', which give access to publicly supplied basic goods such as health and education services, water, and free or subsidized food rations. Both types are potentially severely affected by war.

At the *macro-level* of the national economy, GNP is likely to fall, ie total output of goods and services will fall as a result of war damage and loss of manpower, which is liable to hit agriculture first, especially in a civil war, and reduced foreign exchange earnings from exports (especially where sanctions are in play). Diversion of imports to military expenditure further reduces the foreign exchange available for economic uses. In international wars the reduced exports may be worsened by embargoes; in civil wars reduced food production may be particularly acute. But even without these special conditions reduced production of exports and food is likely as a result of general shortages of inputs and their diversion to war efforts. Entitlements are threatened by the loss in production among the self-employed farmers, falls in available employment, and the reduced real wages which often accompany the escalating inflation.

At the *meso level* of government expenditure allocations there is a downward pressure on tax revenue and expenditure, partly due to falling GNP and partly to reduced efforts to collect tax. Government expenditure on social and economic sectors may be particularly badly hit because of diversion to military expenditure. The social sectors are likely to receive a declining share of a declining total just when their needs for reconstruction and guaranteed minimum food entitlements are rising. As war proceeds, governments are likely to accumulate sharply rising debt, both foreign and domestic, as loans are incurred to pay for the war. Servicing this debt will eat further into the budget, reducing resources available for social needs.

At the *micro level*, households suffer multiple blows – from reduced entitlements among their productive members, from a reduced proportion of earnings when the main wage earner is drafted into the military, killed or injured, and from the reduced ability of the government to provide social services and social safety nets. Preventative health efforts can collapse in war areas so that disease spreads rapidly often with fatal effects, particularly if food entitlements have been severely reduced. Household members may also suffer psychological shock as a result of the many traumatic events that occur during war, including rape, pillage and witnessing relations being killed.

These three factors interact with one another in a way that can lead to massive civilian death during war, as well as widespread destitution among the population.

Development costs

The 'development costs' of war consist of destruction of existing capital, in all its senses, and reductions in new investment. Capital here means physical infrastructure (the transport system, irrigation, power supplies and factories) and social infrastructure (schools and clinics) as well as human capital (people who are killed or migrate), institutional capital (extension services, banks, marketing links, scientific and technical institutions) and, perhaps most critically, social and cultural capital in the form of trust and social cohesion, respect for work and for property. These are all vital for the functioning of society and the economy.

In addition to this damage, wars typically reduce both public and private investment due to competing claims on a declining revenue base; to reductions in perceived returns and, especially, higher risks. Governments tend to cut investment as a result of the general reduction in public resources and the special expenditure demands of war. Aid agencies may reduce aid generally and investment especially, believing that there is little point in building up infrastructure if it is liable to be destroyed, although in some contexts aid may be increased to support the war effort. Private investors reduce their expenditures because of depressed expectations about the economy and profitability and the risks of destruction.

Many factors affect the scale and even the direction of these various human and developmental costs. These include first, the pre-existing socio-economic conditions, and especially the size and nature of 'vulnerable' population sectors who are likely to be most adversely affected. Second, of course, the nature and duration of the war is crucial. Finally, the responses of international agencies and of a country's particular trading and creditor nations can also be critically important.

A study of the 16 worst affected countries

To see what happens in reality and using the somewhat limited available mortality estimates, we identified the 16 countries worst affected by war, where over 0.5 per cent of the 1990 population are estimated to have died directly and indirectly as a result of war between 1970 and 1990. We then analysed the (albeit limited) economic data available for these countries, which were: Afghanistan, Angola, Cambodia, El Salvador, Ethiopia-Eritrea, Guatemala, Iran, Iraq, Lebanon, Liberia, Mozambique, Nicaragua, Somalia, Sudan, Uganda, and Vietnam.[1]

Human costs

In all of the countries for which data are available per capita income fell over the 1980s. The worst performers were Mozambique, Liberia, Nicaragua, Afghanistan, Guatemala and 1970s Uganda. Apart from a number of African countries, which also had negative growth, all performed significantly worse than their regional averages. Per capita food production fell in all but two of them, with six countries showing declines greater than 15 per cent. Food production in Cambodia fell by more than half. Export volumes declined in all but one (Iran); and most showed (smaller) declines in imports. Several countries had very high budget deficits, but some recorded quite low and falling deficits. Inflationary pressures were also uneven. Foreign aid flows were generally increased by the conflict but also varied widely. Mozambique, Somalia, Sudan, Uganda and Ethiopia received massive aid in relation to imports but Iran and Iraq virtually none. The significance of these data, however, is not so much in the negative effects they record as in the degree of variation between countries. The most negative effects occurred in countries with long-lasting and geographically pervasive civil wars, where rebels were well supplied from outside and instructed to reap maximum damage on the economy (ie Mozambique, Nicaragua and Afghanistan).

At the meso-policy level during war, very different strategies can occur. Nicaragua and probably Mozambique were able to increase revenue-raising capacity as a proportion of GNP and to bring extremely high public expenditure levels (with high budget deficits) to bear on the war effort. This might be characterized as the fairly effective policy response of radical socialism to external destabilization (in the type four scenario). More typically, however, revenue fell by a small proportion of GNP as the government found it more difficult to raise revenue (Guatemala, Sudan, El Salvador and Ethiopia). At the other extreme, some governments virtually lost revenue-raising capacity either through spoil or thieving, corrupt politics (type three) or the disintegration into 'war lord' politics (type five) in which the government machine gives way to anarchy.

The degree to which states could direct GNP to military expenditure varied widely. It was over 20 per cent in Angola, Nicaragua and Iraq, and over 10 per cent in Ethiopia and Mozambique, but in most military expenditure was relatively low (below 3 per cent of GNP). Surprisingly, perhaps, there was no general relationship between high military expenditure during war and relatively lower expenditure upon health and services. Countries in our case study able to maintain state revenues tried to finance both military and public service requirements. In Iran and Nicaragua the proportion of government expenditure directed at social services actually increased during the war. All five states with the highest proportions of GNP directed to military expenditure also had active food intervention policies that served remarkably well to maintain entitlements given the degree of economic rupture in large parts of the countryside. In other states, social service provision was hit drastically by war. In Somalia, for example, expenditure on health and education fell from 11 per cent of the government budget to less than 3 per cent. Like several other governments (including Sudan), the Somali state also failed to maintain food security through subsidies, price controls and public distribution systems with drastic consequences. Coherent and activist states are thus central in helping to moderate the human costs of war.

At the household level enormous disruptions occurred, including high rates of mortality and injury to key income earners (both civilians and combatants). In some countries, this was also the result of massive mine laying. Vietnam had around one million widows and 800,000 orphans and Afghanistan an estimated 700,000 widows. Forced migration within and beyond national boundaries occurred to varying degrees. Around half of the populations of Afghanistan, Angola and Mozambique were displaced, and around one quarter in El Salvador. These displacements typically reflected a complex and varied set of factors, both security and livelihood.

The process of war often leads to household disintegration as heads of household are killed, mobilized or migrate in search of food. Only in Nicaragua did government policy during civil war permit a maintenance of welfare in the most war affected regions and hence there were relatively low rates of migration. In several countries violence was so pervasive that large proportions of children reported witnessing or experiencing murder or torture, with as yet still little understood long-term effects. Absolute poverty with massive food deficits following conflict was most marked in African countries which started off already particularly poor. Declines in health and welfare variables were widespread in Africa, but in Middle Eastern and Latin American countries declines were less marked – sometimes improvements were actually registered.

The damaging effects of war often reflect principally the loss of rights experienced by civilians in relation to authority (state or rebel) and the military, and the individuals or groups who are able to use the power of these institutions for their own ends. Loss of freedom of movement, looting, irregular taxation, forced labour and abuse of all kinds are the norm for civilians in war zones, at times by 'friend' and 'foe' alike.

Development costs

The developmental costs associated with war also varied markedly. In many countries there was severe destruction of agricultural, transport, service and commercial infrastructure, seen most dramatically in Afghanistan, Mozambique and Angola. In Mozambique, a quarter of the health centres and 40 per cent of primary schools were destroyed during 1982-86. Investment during conflict has ranged from quite high in Mozambique to extremely low in Uganda. The flight of skilled labour was somewhat uneven: Nicaragua and Uganda lost particularly large sections of the professional classes. What happens to administrative and service institutions during wars – in both the rebel and government held zones – has varied markedly, from a blossoming of them in rebel-held Eritrea, to an almost complete collapse.

These costs do not fall equally on men and women. In many situations, women bear the brunt of the costs of war, and receive less support from government institutions than before the conflict. However, the limited research available suggests that women are often able to take some advantage from the sweeping changes in values and social structures that occur in war, because they have less to lose than men from the destruction of the old ways of life and social order. More research is required to understand these gender impacts.

A SYNTHESIS FOR ACTION

Our analysis shows that the economic impacts of serious wars are not uniformly disastrous, but extraordinarily varied between countries. These differences reflect the pre-existing socio-economic conditions, the nature of the conflict, and the policy measures that governments and international relief programmes pursued.

States involved in international conflicts such as border wars or foreign aggression can often galvanize national will and increase taxation (and budget deficits) to increase social and developmental expenditures alongside an increased military budget. But when the adversary is too powerful or persistent, the over-extended state may collapse both economically and politically. A country then slides into disintegration when formal government cannot re-emerge because national resources have been plundered or appropriated by 'war lords'. Such a collapse can also result from a spiral of 'spoil politics', where a succession of different cliques use military means to capture state power and then loot and/or inefficiently distribute national resources under patronage. These cases do not emerge suddenly; they develop from historic events which occur over time, often a prolonged civil war. Early support for policies to reinforce government structures from outside might prevent this anarchy developing. Once near anarchy has developed, a first priority is to flood the country with food, so food supplies are sufficient and the 'food weapon', where one faction denies food to a part of the country, is made ineffectual. A second priority is to reinstate a government strong enough and with sufficient revenue to guarantee entitlements. Sometimes this may be best achieved by supporting local government structures.

The way international financial institutions and bilateral donors respond to conflicts can crucially affect their outcomes, as well as the well-being of the civilians involved. Neglect is one form of policy. The imposition of 'structural adjustment' packages, insensitive to the demands of a war situation, is another. Structural adjustment programmes typically involve reduction in government expenditure, especially food subsidies, and reduced or eliminated price controls. These measures can have particularly harmful effects during war as they permit food prices to escalate and make it even more difficult to protect essential health and education services.

These packages reduce the capacity of the state to ameliorate developmental and welfare threats, and can further promote conflict by undermining national politico-economic integration and state authority. The Bretton Woods institutions (The World Bank and IMF) clearly need to reappraise their structural adjustment programmes in general, but particularly in countries at war. Likewise, the approach of international and non-governmental agencies, which tend to undermine state coherence by establishing parallel structures and uneven activity, also needs to be reassessed. Increased state management of the economy, systematic intervention to secure welfare, short-term borrowing, and a drive to increasing state revenues, are all central features of successful strategies in handling the impact of war. This is true whether in Europe's world wars of yesterday, or today's African insurgencies.

How relief is provided can greatly affect the impact and outcomes of wars. In some countries at war, relief aid comes to dominate the economy totally (eg Mozambique and Somalia), and its management and distribution becomes central to national and local politics. Donors are aware that their interventions directly influence the balance of military power between government and rebel forces. Frequently general economic aid or relief food is diverted to direct military ends. Sometimes donors may welcome this as part of their foreign policy agendas, or because support for the local military can mean a more secure and settled existence for the civilians under their control. International agencies have been notoriously bad at resolving what kinds of impact they should have on national and state institutional capacity and on achieving these through coherent coordinated policies. The provision or withholding of aid is also a major carrot and stick used by the international community to press for peace agreements of particular kinds – although whether or not this works is doubtful. However, the short- and long-term impacts that this can have on the ground are important. Competition over the control of relief aid may easily become the focus of damaging conflicts between a variety of civilian and military factions. It may even contribute to disintegration of one or both parties to the conflict into forms of 'war lord' politics (eg Southern Sudan in the 1990s).

For civilians in war zones, and indeed for refugees, the greatest determinant of their well-being is not the quantity of relief aid, but the degree to which they retain rights to livelihood and welfare. During wars, states and their agents increase their power over their citizens, particularly those deemed to be of the enemy group. Furthermore, administrative officials, economic elites and soldiers find great opportunities to exploit and control civilians for their own ends. Relief agencies can play as important a role in protecting civilians' rights as they can in providing relief. The strategies used to achieve this, however, have to reflect the causes of conflict: whether there is an overly strong state, an over-extended state, a partisan state or a disintegrated state.

The variations in performance of countries involved in wars point to both the possibility and the importance of government policy to sustain food entitlements and preventative health services during war. To avoid indirect deaths governments must have as a central objective the maintenance of minimum market entitlements. However, the exclusive use of the market to allocate resources and determine prices and incomes is highly dangerous during war, because it can result in a collapse of market entitlements for large numbers of people in a very short time. War creates special dangers because it can lead to sudden changes in production, employment and prices.

A variety of policies are needed to maintain entitlements, including food rations and subsidies, employment schemes, infant and child monitoring and feeding through health centres and pension schemes. These policies may be carried out singly or in combination. Each may be targeted to reduce costs, but efficient targeting usually requires a strong administrative structure that may not be feasible and often excludes large numbers of people in need. Maintaining and extending publicly provided health services, particularly immunization and the treatment of diarrhoea, are an essential supplement to adequate food entitlements.

Experience is accumulating that the policy of not making developmental interventions during wars is usually flawed. First, because it raises the long-term costs of war – especially serious when war is prolonged. Second, such developmental interventions are often essential if relief is to be effective, for example through the maintenance of adequate transport systems. In any case, programmes that provide people with productive employment rather than providing hand-outs are usually much more efficient as well as humane. Similar arguments have long been recognized for refugees, even if these arguments have been little heeded. However, development programmes during wars would have to be designed somewhat differently – both to minimize the danger of destruction and loss of investment and to focus on the unique constraints and opportunities.

Development efforts are a 'waste of resources' only if any new projects are likely to be destroyed immediately. One way of avoiding this is to redesign the development efforts so that they are less vulnerable to attack, for example, building minor, untarmacked roads, small airstrips, mobile schools and health posts, mini-energy projects, rather than massive projects which are obvious targets; and building small-scale, dispersed industry rather than large centralized factories. Maintaining development programmes and reconstruction can also be crucial for morale and the legitimacy of the state. This is particularly important for countering wars of destabilization/foreign aggression and in situations of state disintegration.

Understanding the contrasts between types of wars and states can help in deciding whether support to state largesse is likely to be effective in reducing military conflict and its effects in the longer term. Those countries that managed to maintain or increase aggregate revenue during their wars (namely Mozambique, Nicaragua, Vietnam, Iran and Iraq) could maintain social services and an investment capacity which reduced developmental costs and assisted post-war reconstruction. However these states have not been able to achieve political stability. In part this reflects an international environment hostile to independent-minded Third World states, but also the strains imposed by the aggressive all-encompassing state – the kind of regime that can further advance its claims on its citizens in the face of general hardship and violence. Yet in states riven by wars over 'spoil-politics', one reason for the destructive struggles over control of government is the extent to which political office guarantees access to national resources for diversion and redistribution to those holding power. The challenge to new leadership in these states is how to make economic necessities politically viable in a situation where the World Bank/IMF and donors provide an impossible strait-jacket of fiscal policies. The threat of a collapse into 'war lord' stagnation is all too clear in many African states where the state has become impossibly weakened. Recovery from such a collapse is very difficult: even Museveni's achievements in Uganda still leave a very precarious state.

In our view, an understanding of the relationship between the nature and capacity of states and the form of military conflict they are embroiled in, would enable policy makers to design economic policies that can minimize the human costs of the war, reduce the forces causing conflict, and maximize wartime welfare and post-war economic resurgence. Such new thinking in economics, however, should be coupled with ways to tackle the new levels of weapons availability and the legacies of military might and political disjuncture in many countries of the South.

A CASE STUDY: MOZAMBIQUE

Mozambique illustrates how devastating the welfare and developmental costs of sustained warfare can be and how far governmental policy can mitigate those effects. It also illustrates how international aid generally failed to respond to the country's crisis with a coordinated and rational long-term strategy to minimize these costs.[2]

Mozambique was a revolutionary 'socialist' state that fell victim to external destabilization and, to a lesser extent, to a variety of internal opposition (a type four scenario). There was an initial period of fairly effective state response to the economic damage from the war (late 1970s to mid-1980s), followed by a trend to the state being overwhelmed by the extent of destruction. Its capacity to respond coherently was further undermined by the nature of international aid (late 1980s to the cease-fire of October 1992). This led to an increasingly 'type five' situation of militarized disintegration where the ability of state or aid agencies to intervene to support people's short- or long-term livelihood was progressively lost.

In Mozambique, the war was fought largely without front lines, and, for over a decade, in almost every district of the country. Few villages were unaffected, and most of the rural administrative centres changed hands several times. Only the provincial cities never fell to the rebel forces (the MNR or Renamo). This maximized war damage – both in immediate human and developmental terms. Basically, the war led to catastrophic economic losses overall, halving GNP and destroying most of the productive assets in the state, peasant and commercial sectors. Hundreds of thousands of people, possibly more than a million, lost their lives from the indirect effects of war (especially through the destruction of primary health provision); and more than 100,000 were probably deliberately killed or starved during the fighting.

The Frelimo government initially worked hard to maintain services and to meet welfare needs in the countryside, initially sustaining government revenue and management. But by the late 1980s its efforts were overwhelmed by the extent of the problems and the size of the reduction in the national economy and hence in total state revenue. The government tried to deal with this by borrowing heavily and unsustainably (soon owing two to three times its GNP). Though this cushioned the war's impact initially, the Mozambique government then had to accept from 1987 structural adjustment in return for debt interest rescheduling and World Bank-brokered international aid. Military expenditure reached half of the state budget by the late 1980s, and, in the face of restrictions imposed by structural adjustment on borrowing for service provision, spending in areas like health was reduced substantially. Despite government attempts to preserve entitlements of the existing urban poor and the one million plus people displaced into urban centres, such measures achieved less than they could have because of the economic instability caused by the war and structural adjustment, and the basic donor hostility to such programmes. In practice, attempts to support rural populations became restricted to an internationally-funded emergency relief programme for an official 'two million' internally displaced (a figure determined basically by donor funds).

For political and technical reasons, international aid could not address the fundamental issues in Mozambique's short- or long-term stability. The US$500 million donated every year since the late 1980s for the emergency in Mozambique and the nearly two million refugees in neighbouring countries was approximately double the government's military expenditure at its 1986-90 peak. Clearly, as was widely recognized, allocating even limited amounts of such funds to the logistically incapacitated Mozambique military would have had much greater welfare benefits by protecting civilians *in situ* rather than attempting to assist people once attacked and driven out of their homes by Renamo. A few aid projects and commercial initiatives amply demonstrated the benefits of a (non-lethal) military aid component or private militia presence but most donors and agencies were shy of such activities. They were even prepared to see millions of dollars of donor investment destroyed by Renamo raids for want of minor support to government garrisons. Furthermore, agencies simply watched desperate government troops, who received neither reliable salary nor logistical support, turn increasingly to commandeering their relief provisions and to raiding or taxing peasant or displaced populations. Admittedly the level of corruption in the Ministry of Defence made logistical support of the soldiers through central government difficult, but it would have been possible for much imaginative action at district level.

Not only could civilians in the war zones have benefited more from non-lethal military aid than from emergency assistance in the camps for refugees and displaced people, but also the national economy could have benefited considerably from spending in defence of its assets. The annual US$500 million of emergency aid was only half or less of the economic costs of the war itself in terms of reductions in GNP. Thus, international investment in maintaining government defence of the country's productive peasantry and infrastructural assets would also have had a high rate of return in economic terms. This was, of course, one of the things that the Mozambique government recognized in its own borrowing for the military, borrowing that eventually was largely curtailed by the World Bank and IMF.

Although donors were shy of supporting the Frelimo government's defensive capacity, very few agencies explored the options for providing relief or development assistance through rebel Renamo structures. In part this was because, whatever their attitude towards Frelimo's 'socialism', donors understood that long-term viability depended upon the government surviving until the Renamo rebels accepted peace negotiations. It also reflected the way emergency aid to the governments of the Mozambique and other 'frontline states' was used by western donors as a sop to blunt criticism of their failure to tackle South Africa's blatant regional destabilization policies. As a result, no comparable budget lines were available for work in rebel zones, and for many years people under Renamo control were denied assistance or support in a war of attrition where the donors were unwilling to make a decisive intervention. Ironically, this very factor was later used to the advantage of the peace process. By 1992, war and drought had reduced the Renamo-held zones to such levels of famine that even the military could not sustain itself, and first an agreement on humanitarian corridors and then a final cease-fire were in part built on the promise of relief for these zones.

Political sensitivities prevented donors from responding to the clearly primarily military cause and solution to Mozambique's destabilization and then drift towards militarized disintegration. There was a parallel failure of the aid programmes to support the kind of state coherence that was necessary to resist further collapse and to sustain the population. Despite the dedication and wisdom of a number of donors and agencies and the valuable contribution of certain programmes, the overall effects of aid fell far short of what could have been achieved. Contradictory and often competitive policies were followed by different donors and agencies. Where they were prepared to direct resources through state structures, they often ended up funding more than one government unit to do the same thing. Trapped in an over-ambitious professional framework and with the loss of political direction, under-paid officials in the ill-resourced ministries lost much of the will to work and sought other means of livelihood. Key central governmental units withered under these internal and external pressures. Even where donors recognized the impending disastrous consequences of this, for example in the case of the government's relief unit, they simply lacked the political will to do anything about it, thus jeopardizing hundreds of thousands of lives and destroying even their own ability to operate effectively.

Donors providing emergency assistance failed to explore how they might mitigate the long-term consequences of the war by supporting key state institutions and programmes in human resources development. It was abundantly clear for several years before the cease-fire that the refusal of donors to support certain state structures with recurrent expenditure was not only harmful in the short term, but would have dire consequences for post-war reconstruction. For the beleaguered Ministry of Education, in particular, this meant not only another generation with little education in a country with critical skilled manpower shortages, but also that enormously costly institution-building would be required to repair the continuing loss of trained and skilled staff. A relatively small amount of support for recurrent expenditure in the short term would have yielded great returns in the long term. Despite some structural problems within the Ministry, the real constraints on donor assistance were the combination of the current unfashionability of education in the fickle aid business, and the general hostility towards meeting state recurrent expenditures whatever the logical outcomes of this.

The impact of aid programmes' failure to support state welfare and developmental provision extended beyond its direct affect on people's well-being to the wider security situation. As the state became less able to deliver services it contributed to the loss of morale and state legitimacy which rendered the country more vulnerable to the Renamo rebels. This lack of political strength combined with economic weakness (compounded by the withdrawal of existing logistical support for the military from the ex-Communist bloc after 1990) meant that even once Renamo's military capacity was greatly reduced the government forces could not effectively dislodge them from the countryside. Thus, the war dragged on until both sides saw that they had lost. Given the wrecked state of the rural economy, the focus of political struggle shifted to the allocation of new external resources under an internationally brokered peace agreement.

Local studies, however, suggest that the pattern of interactions between relief assistance, military stability and economic recovery are much more complicated than this general view suggests. Work in Zambezia by Ken Wilson and Jovito Nunes suggests that, at least in the important centres of Milange and Mocuba, the emergency programmes *did* have positive developmental impacts. Ironically, their positive contribution to peasant livelihood by improving security and economic activity was primarily though the effects of 'corruption'. Although one or two ngos supported district level structures, most relief was exclusively targeted at the displaced and returnees in conditions where the state structures and military were starved of resources. Fortunately government officials and the military diverted part of the relief aid and used it to supplement their totally inadequate salaries so that they could do their jobs effectively and keep the areas secure against Renamo encroachment. Furthermore, this 'diversion' of relief items stimulated the emergence of commerce which in turn generated and profited from peasant wage labour and other economic activity. Such independent commercial activity actually became central to physical and economic reconstruction, and was much more effective in enabling peasants to re-establish sustainable livelihoods than the agencies' direct programmes. To cap it all, by late 1991, at least in Milange, it was this emergent commercial community who were taxing themselves to provide the army with logistics for the defence of the town, and which thus expanded the secure zone for economic activity under government forces. Obviously, the agencies could have made a much more effective contribution to civil authority and military logistics by contributing directly to their work than that which was achieved through the uneven and semi-clandestine system of corruption.

Clearly, international relief donors have to consider how they should work with the state, what effects this has for stability and what contributes best to the immediate and long-term welfare of the war-torn population.

3

The Development Trap: Militarism, Environmental Degradation and Poverty in the South

Nadir Abdel Latif Mohammed

Developing countries have made great efforts to speed the process of socio-economic progress in the post-colonial era, often with very ambitious development programmes. However, after many decades of national rule and planning many countries have failed to achieve their development objectives.

To explain this failure we need to be clear about the concept of development. A precise definition for socio-economic development is difficult, although countries can be easily classified into developed and developing categories.[1] Development is a multi-dimensional and dynamic process. It requires high levels of per capita income as well as an egalitarian distribution of income, elimination of poverty and the provision of human basic needs, but without jeopardizing the needs and prospects of future generations. The need is to achieve *sustainable* development: development that ensures rapid economic growth, equal distribution of income, without degrading the environment or jeopardizing the right of future generations to achieve progress and prosperity. Economic growth is thus a necessary but not sufficient condition in itself for development, which also involves social transformation and meeting non-material requirements such as the ability of individuals to participate in economic and political decision making.[2]

Various indicators show the failure of developing countries to achieve development. For example, the rate of growth of real GDP per capita in developing countries fell from 3.9 per cent in 1965–1973 to 2.5 per cent in 1973–1980 and 1.6 per cent in the 1980–1989 period. In sub-Saharan Africa and Latin America during that period, the growth rate of real GDP per capita went backwards, falling to −1.2 per cent and −0.04 per cent respectively. Child mortality in South Asia exceeds 170 per thousand; life expectancy in sub-Saharan Africa is 50 years; and more than 110 million children in developing countries lack access to primary education.

Development economists point to various obstacles to Third World development. These include:

- political instability;
- lack of basic infrastructure;
- inadequacy of well-developed human resources and managerial skills
- unfair terms of trade with the developed world;
- scarcity of natural resources;
- faulty development policies and planning; and
- military intervention and civil wars.[3]

This chapter pinpoints three pivotal factors which inhibit socio-economic development: militarization, environmental degradation, and poverty. Not only do these factors make a large contribution to underdevelopment, but each is also both a consequence and cause of the others. The links between them produce a *development trap* for most developing countries. This chapter explores the interlinkages and feedbacks of these three factors and their direct and indirect effects on socio-economic development, with special emphasis on the African continent. Finally, it looks at possible ways out of the trap, in particular at prospects for military conversion.

POVERTY TRENDS

Poverty refers to the inability to attain a minimum standard of living. This minimum standard of living (the poverty line) requires, according to World Bank estimates, an annual income of $370. On this basis, more than one billion people in developing countries – one-fifth of the world's population – are living in poverty.[4] The largest number of poor people in 1985 were in South Asia, with over 500 million (about half the population), followed by a further 280 million in East Asia, 210 million in China and 180 million in sub-Saharan Africa. Each year the population increases in size, but the amount of natural resources with which to sustain them, and to eliminate poverty, remains finite.

The high poverty levels of the last two decades are likely to increase in the 1990s for many reasons. First, the Third World's prospects of economic recovery in the 1990s are gloomy due to such problems as debt, world recession and political instability. Second, the population growth rates of most developing countries exceed the rates of GDP growth, and so per capita income will fall in absolute terms. Finally, within countries, poverty has also been exacerbated by the unequal distribution of land and other assets.

MILITARIZATION TRENDS

Militarization is the process of expansion of the military establishment within a society. It can be quantified by a set of economic, political and strategic indicators such as the level of military expenditure and its shares in government expenditure and total GDP, as well as by arms imports, size of the armed forces, and military intervention in the political scene.

Throughout the past five decades, the world has consistently devoted between 4.5 and 7 per cent of global GNP and more than 15 per cent of governmental expenditures to military expenditure. According to a 1983 American study, well over 70 million people were then engaged, directly or indirectly, in military activities. In 1988, world military expenditures exceeded one trillion dollars, world armed forces numbered 28 million and total world arms transfers reached $49 billion.[5] From 1965 to 1985, Third World military expenditure was about 15 per cent of the world total but it accounted for more than 15 per cent of total government expenditure in the developing countries. Although the bulk of world military spending was by the developed countries, the fastest growth was among the poorer countries. This trend declined in the late 1980s but was reversed in 1990.[6]

Military intervention in Third World politics has become a universal phenomenon. Inefficiency of civilian administration, the eradication of corruption, and the characteristics of the armed forces as disciplined and modern organizations were the declared reasons behind military interventions. Nevertheless, military governments themselves have failed to achieve political stability, and the frequency of military coups has increased in developing countries, and particularly in Africa. The size of developing countries' military establishments has increased enormously in the post-independence period and the last three decades have witnessed high incidence of bloody internal conflicts and civil wars in individual developing countries. Overall, most developing countries have seen considerable militarization since the Second World War.[7]

ENVIRONMENTAL DEGRADATION TRENDS

The speed of environmental degradation, particularly the environmental problems caused by human activities, is receiving mounting international attention. Climate warming, ozone depletion, loss of biodiversity and acid rain are global concerns.

There are many regional environmental threats too, both in developed and developing countries. These include air and water pollution, lowered capacity of groundwater storage, urban pollution, deforestation, soil erosion and desertification. Although the magnitude of environmental stress in various parts of the world is uneven and uncertain, most of this degradation is irreversible.

MAKING THE LINKS

Poverty, environmental degradation and militarization are inextricably linked. If we start with poverty, for example, we find poor people are usually forced to put pressure on their local environment for survival; environmental degradation and competition over natural resources results, which in turn gives rise to social tension and armed conflicts; higher militarization (and consequently high military spending) follows armed conflicts. Higher military expenditure has substantial economic costs, particularly on economic growth, which is needed to combat poverty. This in turn leads to more widespread poverty and the development trap is re-enforced.

If we start with militarization, however, we find that armed conflicts and military establishments are highly polluting.[8] This leads to environmental degradation that jeopardizes economic growth due to the depletion of resources. However, economic deprivation and poverty are most often the main causes of social tension and armed conflict and the trap is again re-enforced.

Poverty and environmental degradation

Poverty contributes greatly to environmental stress, which itself leads to increasing the levels of penury (the so-called *poverty trap*). Poor people tend to rely on natural resources for their survival and are often forced to overuse environmental resources to survive. This impoverishing of the environment in turn threatens their survival further. In many poorer countries, agriculture, forestry and energy production generate half of the GNP and the export of natural resources contributes substantially to export earnings. Thus their prevailing economic activities contribute directly to resource depletion and environmental degradation in most developing countries. Deforestation, for example, is causing increasingly destructive floods in Asia, and desertification in large parts of Africa and Latin America. In the African Sahel, deforestation followed by soil erosion has turned vast areas of land into deserts. Furthermore, in poor communities the increasing demand for firewood leads to deforestation, or to the use of dry cow dung for fuel which deprives the soil of nutrients. Thus soil fertility declines and the poverty circle closes tighter.[9]

The World Commission on Environment and Development (WCED) in their report *Our Common Future* argued in 1987 that 'those who are poor and hungry will often destroy their immediate environment to survive; they will cut down forests; their livestock will overgraze grass land; they will overuse marginal lands; and in growing numbers they will crowd into congested cities'. Rural-urban migration puts more pressure on the environment in cities as well as the countryside.[10] Some degraded systems may recover, but the loss of just one inch of top soil may take nature centuries to replace. Poor societies are unable to overcome the negative effects they produce, unlike rich communities which have access to funds and technical know-how to absorb the wastes they produce.

Rapid population growth also puts more pressure on the environment and reduces the environment's ability to dilute the wastes produced. Instead, the residuals from production and consumption simply accumulate. Market failures in developing countries are a further cause of environmental degradation. On many occasions, environmental resources are treated as 'free goods'. Some economists also argue that the falling real incomes of poor farmers leads them to overuse natural resources.

Nonetheless, although poverty contributes to environmental degradation, so too do industrialization and the industrialized nations, particularly in relation to the global environment threats.

The environmental limits to growth

It is now well recognized that the environment affects economic growth and development. During the 1960s and early 1970s, many people argued that zero growth of the economy and the population was necessary to avoid the disastrous transgression of the physical 'outer limits' of the planet. The emergence of the concept of *sustainable development* in the 1970s, however, changed this position. The United Nations Environment Programme (UNEP) then introduced the concept of *ecodevelopment,* defined as 'development at regional and local levels... consistent with the potentials of the area involved, with attention given to the adequate and rational use of the natural resources, and to applications of technological styles ... and organizational forms that respect the natural ecosystem and local sociocultural patterns'.[11]

Clearly the flow of natural resources such as water, forests and energy, into production and consumption activities is crucial for most productive activities in developing countries and their availability determines the potential for growth. This constraint on growth is particularly binding for those developing countries that rely on the export of primary products. It tends to be seen in the form of rising costs and diminishing returns, rather than in a sudden loss of a resource base.[12]

Many investment projects cause environmental damage, particularly those in infrastructure, industry and even agriculture. They are likely to use new, more expensive, technologies, equipment and management techniques than the earlier ones. Safeguarding the environment may also require still more expensive choices and development options as countries approach the ecological and physical limits to the use of land and mineral resources.

The industries most heavily reliant on environmental resources and the most heavily polluting are growing most rapidly in developing countries, where there is both more urgency for growth and less capability to minimize damaging side effects. Energy generation in developing countries usually involves environmental degradation or resource depletion. Opposition to the depletion of resources and the absence of other viable energy options usually delays energy projects, which are crucial for growth and development.

Militarization and poverty

The concept of militarization is very wide but I focus here on a specific aspect: the direct effects of military establishments on the economy and the environment. This includes the army during peace (its finance, weapons and equipment) and its effect during war (finance, destruction, etc). The effects of the political aspects of militarization (eg military intervention in politics) are not included.

Military establishments in developing countries play a complex role in the development process because of the prevailing high militarization levels and the continuous military intervention in economic and political activities. A rapidly rising military expenditure, particularly in Africa, has been accompanied by poor economic performance, poverty, and escalating wars and conflicts. Thus the relationship between military expenditure and development has become a relevant policy issue and area of study.

Unfortunately the economic impact of military expenditure in developing countries has been relatively neglected despite a remarkable growth in studies dealing with its impact in developed countries. However, the publication of data on military expenditure by some international organizations and the escalating trends of these expenditures in many developing countries in the last two decades have motivated quite a few empirical studies on the economic impact of military expenditure in developing countries.

The economic impact of military expenditure

Economic theory does not offer obvious predictions and postulates on the impact of military expenditure on growth and development, because economic theories do not provide a unique role for military expenditure as a distinctive economic activity. Even so, various connections can be identified. The emphasis in this section is on the impact of military spending on macro-economic variables, and economic growth in developing countries, particularly in Africa, rather than on economic development. This is because growth can be quantified and is a necessary but not sufficient condition for development.

Military expenditure influences economic growth through many channels, both directly and indirectly. Some major channels include the indirect effects on human capital formation, savings and investment, and the balance of payments, as well as the direct growth-stimulating effects. These effects are interdependent and interrelated, but are treated separately here.

On human capital formation

People and their skills (human capital) are an important factor of production. Adequate human capital (including managerial, entrepreneurial and technical personnel) may increase the productivity of physical capital such as money, plant and machinery. In developing countries, a major obstacle to rapid economic growth has been the lack of skilled and educated people (well-developed human capital). Although the relationship between military expenditure and human capital formation is very complex, military spending can influence it directly by generating employment, increasing the supply of skilled labour, and indirectly through its effect on government spending on education and health.

Certainly the military mobilizes labour and offers employment. In most developing countries, soldiers come from villages and rural agricultural sectors, where they are either unemployed or underemployed, or do not have access to employment centres. These employment benefits to the economy are, however, limited by two considerations. First, only a small proportion of the population enters the army; and second, the military also frequently employs skilled labour, which is in short supply in most developing countries, and hence, reduces the amount available for civilian production.

Some economists argue that the military is an important source of technical and administrative skills which can subsequently be of use to the civilian economy and so stimulate growth.[13] It is also often argued that the organizational skills and modern attitudes and aptitudes of the military tend to break up social rigidities which inhibit human capital formation in developing countries. While the military does teach many skills, from driving and repairing vehicles, metal and woodworking, construction and improved agricultural techniques, to engineering and other sciences, especially in volunteer armies, these spin-offs should not be exaggerated.[14] Some of the skills taught in the army are military-specific and expensive, while the military often competes with the civilian sector for other scarce specialities (such as physicians and engineers). The transferability of skills is also not automatic because the trained personnel will not be available to the civilian sector for a large portion of their working life, particularly in the many developing countries with volunteer armies. There is also no reason why the military should be intrinsically more modern than other civilian institutions in removing social rigidities.

Military expenditure affects human capital formation mainly through its impact on government spending on education. Given that both military and education spending come from the public purse and the upper limit on developing countries' budgets, there may be a one-to-one trade-off between military and education expenditures. Consequently, increases in military outlays may hinder the development of human resources by limiting the education budget.[15] Although the military provides independently services such as training, education and health, as one researcher concluded: 'Had some portion of the funds devoted to military training been directed towards civil-sector manpower formation, there can be no doubt that a larger number of people could have acquired skills directly useful to the civil economy'.[16] In some developing countries, increases in military outlays are at the expense of economic and other welfare services rather than education and health spending.[17] Furthermore, if the overall effect of military spending on economic growth is negative, then given the positive connection between growth and human capital formation, military expenditure exerts another indirect negative effect on human capital accumulation.

On the whole, then, the evidence suggests that the employment and technical spin-offs of the military are limited compared with the trade-off between military and education spending and, therefore, military spending has significant adverse effects on human capital formation.

On physical capital

Physical capital accumulation, that is, money available for investment, is an important ingredient in the growth process. It can be affected by military expenditure through a multitude of interrelated channels, but particularly through its impact on domestic savings and investment. In developing countries, this relationship is not straightforward as domestic savings are not automatically translated into productive investment; they might take the form of idle hoarding, be consumed wastefully or conspicuously, or be invested abroad.

Military spending affects the level of domestic savings directly and indirectly, and there is a considerable debate over whether the total impact is positive or negative. In developing countries, where the taxable capacity is limited by the dominance of traditional and subsistence sectors and low income levels, the option of raising revenues from taxation is often not feasible. Budget deficits resulting from increases in military spending are usually financed by expanding the money supply through borrowing from the central bank. This leads to inflation and the impact of inflation on domestic saving is not clear-cut. It may lead to 'forced savings' or higher consumption and lower savings.

Rises in threat perceptions, however, caused by increases in military spending, may reduce savings (that is, by encouraging hoarding). Military expenditure also can reduce saving indirectly if it reduces government expenditures on health and education services and people have to use private savings instead. Overall, in developing countries, military expenditure is likely to reduce the saving propensity.[18]

While military spending can retard savings, this does not mean an equivalent reduction in investment. However, military expenditure can crowd out investment, especially in developing countries where government revenue and expenditure are generally inelastic.[19] In developing countries, supply bottlenecks can also prevent military expenditure from boosting output. In countries which do not produce arms, arms imports compete with imported investment goods for scarce foreign exchange and this hinders investment. Military expenditure can adversely affect human capital formation and this in turn affects the investment potential. Nevertheless, some infrastructural projects built by the military, such as roads or bridges, have spin-offs for the civilian sector but many of these projects are built in remote areas and do not suit civilian production. Overall, there are strong reasons to believe that the effect of military spending on investment is also negative.

On the balance of payments

Military expenditure in an open economy, especially in a non-arms producing country, leads to higher imports and deficits in the trade balance and the balance of payments. A surplus in the trade balance gives a stimulus to growth. The effects of arms imports on the economy depend mainly on the way these imports are financed, whether by outright grants or aid, payment in cash or kind, or credit finance.

In the 1950s and 1960s, outright grants prevailed as superpowers donated weapons to developing countries for political and strategic considerations. Countries which received foreign military aid had a lower burden on their trade balance. However, because of economic and trade difficulties in developed countries, military aid to developing countries has declined rapidly relative to more commercial transactions.

Weapons purchased for cash or kind have serious economic effects. Foreign exchange is very often in short supply in developing countries, and this is made worse by costly arms imports. In Africa, for example, military expenditures set limits to the possibilities of growth. The most immediate effect is the diversion of resources to military installations at the expense of much needed capital goods for development. Clearly, the import of foreign weapons systems does not have any potent economic returns. Shortages in inputs and spare parts caused by shortages of foreign exchange also lead to further erosion of the existing production capacity.

Credit finance has to be paid back in hard currency, and possibly at high interest rates. This means less for investment. Military-related debts are quite substantial and add to the economic burden of weapons imports.[20] More fresh capital is needed to service the existing debt, which causes more foreign exchange shortages, and the 'debt trap' is reinforced.

Arms imports may also reduce savings indirectly because arms imports are usually exempted from imports tariffs and so the government loses revenue. Export capacity can also be reduced by past weapons imports or military expenditures which drew resources from civilian sector investments, again leading to a more precarious balance-of-payments situation.

It is often argued that weapon transfers might have some advantages, including technical spin-offs and the attraction of more economic aid, but the relevance of such spin-offs is questionable and evidence for the correlation between economic aid and military expenditure is weak.[21] Most military assistance programmes to Africa had some built-in destabilizing factors and were responsible for many military coups and resultant political instability.[22] In general military expenditure, and particularly arms imports, is a substantial burden on the balance of payments and economic growth.

On stimulating growth

As well as the various indirect effects of military expenditure on economic growth discussed above, it also has direct effects on growth. According to defence economists, military expenditure stimulates growth directly through increased capacity utilization, for example by increasing employment and demand. There is, however, no agreement on the volume and effectiveness of this. Benefits are probably small in poor countries because such countries' major problems stem from the supply side such as shortages of production inputs, and foreign exchange.

In many developing countries, technological spin-offs and the infrastructure developed by the army might bolster growth. The military may also guarantee a suitable environment for production to proceed by preserving internal stability and security. In African countries, the military engages directly in production activities: crop growing, food manufacturing and even commerce (for instance the Sudanese Military Economic Corporation). The military, many economists have argued, helps in the process of 'modernization' as it inculcates modern attitudes and the work ethos.[23] It also contributes significantly to 'nation building'. These factors are difficult to quantify in economic terms. Also it is important not to confuse the analysis of the economic impact of military expenditure with the impact of military governments on development.

Military expenditure has both direct and indirect effects on economic growth. However, the common simple analogy of the tank–tractor trade-off is not very helpful in understanding its impact because of the complexity and simultaneity of the channels through which these effects operate. Most recent studies have found evidence for the *negative* impact of military expenditure on developing countries' economic growth.[24]

Of four studies that focused on the African continent, one investigated the relationship between military spending and economic growth across 18 African countries for the 1965–1973 period but the results were not statistically significant.[25] Another assessed the impact of military expenditure on industrialization in 26 African countries from 1967 to 1976 and confirmed that military expenditure has an indirect negative impact on GDP manufacturing through both economic and social development factors.[26] A study into the growth-defence relationship for 39 sub-Sahara African countries from 1973 to 1983 found a small negative impact of the defence burden on growth.[27] My own study of 13 sub-Sahara African countries from 1967 to 1985 showed that it is difficult to establish a systematic relationship between military burden and economic variables for the whole sample because the effects of military expenditure on individual countries are different despite the relative homogeneity of the countries chosen.[28] In countries where the military burden was high and increasing, military expenditure had an apparent negative effect on economic growth, investment allocations, and human capital formation, and it contributed to huge balance-of-payments deficits; while in countries with low military burden, the positive spin-offs dominated this negative role. These positive and negative effects were balanced in countries with moderate military burdens and therefore the total effect of military expenditure was negligible and insignificant. The overall evidence does, however, suggest that military spending hinders economic performance in most sub-Sahara African countries.[29]

Some studies found a negative trade-off between education and military spending in developing countries[30] but others concluded that military spending did not have negative consequences for education spending.[31] The discrepancies among these studies reflect the differences in their data bases, country samples and research designs or methods.[32]

Economic conditions and the militarization of society

Most conflict theories stress the importance of economic conditions in explaining conflict and conflict is one important aspect of militarization. For example, Homer-Dixon stressed the importance of economic factors in explaining civil strife and wars and the way different international, regional and national conflicts were motivated by economic factors is well-documented (for example the recent conflict in the Gulf).[33]

Empirical studies on the determinants of military spending confirm the importance of economic factors (such as level of income, government spending) in determining military allocations.[34] In my investigation of 13 sub-Sahara African countries, the differences in the military burdens appear to reflect a complex of economic, political and strategic factors, both at national and international levels. The need to maintain security and stability and to counteract threats was the most important factor in most countries. However, military spending was sensitive to economic conditions and the most important single economic factor was the share of the central government in GDP but not economic growth *per se*.

Most of the military coups in Africa were also said to be motivated by the desire to improve the deteriorating economic conditions, for example in the three successful military interventions in the Sudan in 1958, 1969, and 1989. Food shortages, drought, decrease in agricultural production and shortages in other human basic needs contribute to social tension, and consequently high militarization, of many developing countries. In summary, there are very strong theoretical and empirical grounds for a causal link between militarization (conflict or higher military spending) and economic conditions.

MILITARIZATION AND ENVIRONMENTAL DEGRADATION

The relationship between militarization and the environment has received very little scrutiny. Although some recent studies have shown the negative impact of military establishments and conflicts on the environment, the effect of environmental stress on social tension and conflict needs research. In this section, I focus on the effects of military establishments on the environment first in peacetime and then in war.

Peacetime effects

Armed forces are established to defend national unity and deter foreign aggression. However, many researchers describe them as the 'great polluters' in modern societies. The armed forces contribute, both directly and indirectly, to environmental degradation in many ways.

Direct effects

These include:

- Expropriation of vast areas of land for military training, install-ations and manoeuvres, which could have been used for cultivation or other economic activities. Military activities damage wildlife habitats, forests and soil stability, particularly through the move-ment of heavy and armoured equipment and the discharge of toxic wastes.
- The spread of arms production.[35] The production and testing of conventional weapons generates harmful wastes that cause environmental damage – a situation made worse in the Third World because of minimal safety standards.
- Military establishments are great consumers of resources including petroleum, minerals, chemicals, as well as agricultural products. For example, military aircraft consume half of all aircraft fuel.[36] In addition, arms production is increasingly dependent on non-renewable resources (for example uranium, titanium and chromium).
- Preparation for war, and sometimes routine activities, involves mobilization of forces and a high military presence in certain areas which is usually accompanied by the massing of equipment and arms. This damages local environments and generates extensive wastes (sewage and solids). [37]

- The military share in the destruction of the ozone layer and the greenhouse effect is substantial.

Indirect effects

These include:

- High militarization and military spending, particularly among developing countries, incur substantial economic costs. Their negative impact on economic growth contributes to widespread poverty which is one of the most significant factors threatening environmental security.
- Increases in military spending usually take place at the expense of other categories of government expenditures, which includes environmental conservation projects.
- The military competes with the civilian sector for human resources. Of the total population, only one per cent works in the military sector but more than 20 per cent of all scientists and engineers are employed by the military.[38] The opportunity cost of this human resource capital on the civilian economy and the environment is substantial, particularly in developing countries where the lack of well-developed human capital is perhaps the most significant constraint on economic growth and development.

While the military clearly does contribute to environmental degradation in peacetime, consensus on the volume of such degradation is not universal but it is believed to be more than the military's share in national product.[39] There are, however, some positive effects of militarization on the environment. In many countries, particularly in Africa, the military fight harmful environmental activities such as hunting or cutting down forests. The Kenyan army, for example, has anti-poaching squads for protecting wildlife.

Wartime effects

War causes enormous direct damage to the environment, and puts pressure on the environment indirectly through its displacement of people, who in turn put stress on neighbouring environments.

Modern wars employ defoliants, high explosives, biological agents and weather modification techniques; they also involve land, air, water and space. The use of weapons of mass destruction has grave environmental consequences. Major technological developments have also greatly increased the mobility of conventional arms and the range of their firepower. The Gulf War provides an example of how the destruction of resources (burning oil fields) can be used as a military tool.

Indirect effects include the fact that soldiers and warfare play a significant role in the spread of diseases. There is evidence that war plays a role in the spread of Aids and other sexually transmitted diseases, for example in the geographical pattern of clinical Aids in Uganda.[40]

The effect of environmental factors on militarization

The environment also affects militarization, although the impact of environmental factors on conflict and militarization has received little attention by researchers. Comprehensive human security has two components. *political* security and *environmental* security.[41] Different environmental factors give rise to conflict and, consequently, military actions at the national, regional or international levels. These environmental factors can lead directly to conflict, or indirectly through their effects on other factors.

Direct effects

There are two kinds of environmental threats: those which arise from vandalism, excessive pollution and human intrusion; and those which arise from the non-sustainable utilization of resources. Thus, protecting the environment – and natural and human resources – is one of the most important security goals of all governments.

Competition over natural and scarce resources has been the most important factor in arms races and the outbreak of wars. The World Commission on Environment and Development (WCED) concluded that:

> Environmental stress is both a cause and an effect of political tension and military conflict. Nations have often fought to assert or resist control over raw materials, energy supplies, land, river basins, sea passages, and other key environmental resources. Such conflicts are likely to increase as these resources become scarcer and competition over them increases.[42]

Examples of such resource conflicts include *land* – the Libyan-Chadian conflict over Ozou strip; *raw materials* – the Sudanese-Egyptian conflict over Halayeb area; *energy* – oil supplies from the Gulf; *water* – conflict between Syria and Turkey over the Ataturk dam; and *food* – tribal conflicts in many parts of Africa.

Many countries are already poised for conflict on these issues. It is not a new phenomenon. The quest for territorial expansion to secure resources and trade routes to benefit one or a group of nations has often generated conflict in the past.[43] Environmental conflict arises between countries within the same ecogeographical region (Israel-Jordan, Turkey-Syria, Sudan-Egypt-Ethiopia, Iraq-Iran, Iraq-Kuwait, and so on).

Environmental degradation, pollution, and over-use of common resources such as water, cause conflicts which can lead to wars,[44] or exacerbate conflicts that have other root causes.[45] One example is the direct threat to Syria from the inevitable loading of fertilizers, pesticides and salts that will be transported down the Euphrates as a result of Turkey's agricultural and irrigation efforts in South East Anatolia (GAP) project. These might cause further risks to downstream states (Iraq) and the Gulf ecosystem.[46] Another example is the potential for conflict over the Nile water between Egypt, Sudan and Ethiopia. The present Secretary-General of the United Nations, Dr Boutros Boutros Ghali, warned in the mid-1980s about the potential for conflict here, saying, 'The next war in our region will be over the waters of the Nile, not over politics...'.[47]

Apart from regional conflicts caused by environmental factors, global environmental concerns such as global warming or ozone depletion have an increasing potential for prompting international conflict and are an important factor in international relations.

Indirect effects

Population dislocation and the economic problems caused by environmental degradation are the most important indirect ways in which environmental stress causes social conflict.

Population dislocation caused by environmental change, such as drought or desertification, creates the problem of refugees. If people living in a depleted country see no prospect of feeding themselves they will start to move to better placed areas. This creates a population influx which, in most cases, exceeds the capacity of the host environment and creates conflict and competition over resources. Armed conflict and banditry in western Sudan is an obvious example of this. Political systems may also be threatened by the influx of refugees as they put pressure on the services in cities and cause food shortages. Food riots and urban violence become a danger to national governments, particularly in Africa. Population shifts may also raise the level of tension between countries, for example in Africa where the conflicts between Sudan and Chad, and Sudan and Uganda, in the late 1980s were clearly made worse by environmental refugees crossing interstate boundaries.

Environmental degradation also affects the economy, particularly in Third World countries which depend mainly on natural resources for their exports and local consumption. The WCED emphasized that 'already in parts of Latin America, Asia, the Middle East, and Africa, environmental decline is becoming a source of political unrest and international tension'.[48] People in the affected areas have lower incomes and degrade the environment further in an attempt to survive or move, putting pressure on other communities or cities. This is a cycle of decline which may precipitate tensions, food riots or armed conflicts.

Some researchers are trying to understand these environmental influences on conflict. Homer-Dixon argues that there are seven clusters of environmental problems:

1. greenhouse warming;
2. ozone depletion;
3. deforestation;
4. acid rains;
5. degradation of land;
6. overuse of water supplies; and
7. depletion of fish stocks.

These problems produce four general types of social effect – decrease in economic productivity, changed agricultural production, population displacement, and disruption of institutions and pattern of social behaviour. These in turn lead to three types of conflict: frustration conflicts, identity conflicts and structural conflicts.

Frustration-aggression theories of conflict suggest that people become hostile when they perceive a wide gap between the level of satisfaction that they have achieved and the level they believe they deserve. Group-identity theories explain conflicts involving ethnicity, religion and nationalism: individuals have a need for a sense of belonging that can be satisfied in a group when it attacks or discriminates against another group (for example the Muslim–Hindu conflict in India). Structural theories explain conflicts as arising from the rational calculations of actors in the face of external social or material constraints.[49]

ESCAPING FROM THE DEVELOPMENT TRAP

So far we have discussed the alarming trends of poverty, environmental degradation and militarization in developing countries, their close interlinkages and their re-enforcement on each other. Deteriorating economic conditions can lead to social conflicts and higher militarization; high levels of militarization contribute significantly to environmental degradation; degraded environments limit economic growth and consequently increase the levels of poverty. Conversely, high militarization has a substantial economic cost, restricts economic growth and thus increases poverty; poverty leads to environmental stress and degradation; the environment itself is a major source of conflict (and consequently high militarization). This is what I have called *the development trap*. The great challenge is to find a way out.

All developing countries seek to achieve rapid economic growth and development, to preserve their natural environments, and to secure political stability, national unity and their territories. They need to achieve *sustainable development*. Yet economic development in developing countries cannot be achieved in isolation from international developments. Both national and international policies are recommended here for the realization of sustainable development.

International policies

- The restructuring of global economic relations in such a way that developing countries can obtain the required resources, advanced technology and access to markets, to enable them to pursue a development process that is environmentally sound and also leads to rapid growth to meet the aspirations of their growing populations. The developed countries must contribute through debt relief, increasing economic assistance, technology transfers and new approaches to trade.
- The 'peace dividend' resulting from the end of the Cold War should be used to finance development cooperation and international programmes to respond to global environmental threats.[50]

National policies

- Developing countries should put human rights, democratization of political institutions, and confidence-building measures at the regional level, as their first priority This will reduce both national and regional conflicts which have significantly damaged economic growth and environmental conservation.

- Poverty elimination should receive a very high priority in governments' policies and development plans. Of course the elimination of poverty is not an easy task but there are various strategies available.[51]
- Environmental conservation should be incorporated in all development plans in developing countries. National governments also have to provide adequate environmental education for their populace.
- Population policies in all developing countries are necessary to curb rapid population growth. Improving health services, introducing family planning methods and contraceptives, increasing the age for marriage, and education are all helpful tools to reduce high fertility rates.
- There is a growing need for the *conversion* of military capabilities, personnel, production and technologies.

Most of the above policies are long term. To implement them requires huge resources and a great deal of international cooperation. However, the end of the Cold War, changes in the balance of power between the eastern and western blocs, and the changes in Eastern Europe have provided developing countries with an enormous potential to escape from the vicious development trap by the conversion of military resources and capabilities to civilian uses.

Conversion

The key threats facing the world are poverty, environmental degradation and the growing internal conflicts in Africa, Asia, Eastern Europe and the former Soviet Union. The end of the superpowers' rivalry has provided many Third World countries with opportunities for reducing their military spending levels. This peace dividend should be used to fund a structural adjustment and conversion programme and investments in critical human, environmental and infrastructural needs. The reducing of military spending and conversion has been the subject of considerable research and interest over the years, both in the developed and developing countries.[52]

Despite being a rather vague concept, conversion is commonly understood as 'the transformation of military resources into civil activities and production'.[53] It means more than simply the reduction of military production; it involves a structural rebuilding of the national economy and its productive sectors. Thus conversion is a simultaneous and integral part of arms reduction efforts, because the employment creation potentials of conversion can outweigh the anxieties of unemployment due to arms reduction.

There have been three broad approaches to conversion:[54]

1. *Macroeconomic* – this focuses on the negative relationship between arms spending and economic growth, and emphasizes the macroeconomic benefits from the conversion of the defence industrial base to civilian production. Therefore, cuts in military spending will result in a tangible 'peace dividend'.

2. *Microeconomic* – this focuses on company or plant-based conversion, which involves the re-use or transformation of existing military resources to civilian purposes. A related strategy is diversification, in which defence industries attempt to minimize their vulnerability to defence market fluctuations by engaging in non-military production in addition to their existing military production. This approach has not been particularly successful, partly because of the differences between commercial and military production criteria and cultures. Some suggested reasons for this failure are that microeconomic conversion focuses on products rather than process innovation and this tends to reinforce industrial and technological patterns of production rather than transforming them. As such, it is a missed opportunity for a more broad-based economic restructuring.[55]

3. *Political* – this emphasizes the transformation of resources tied up in defence production within a broader socio-economic and political context. It is not as narrow as the economic approaches, and encompasses the demilitarization of society, for example demobilization and reduced defence expenditure. Conversion is seen as an opportunity or lever to effect changes in the structure of society, and to challenge existing industrial and technological priorities and the social relations of production inherent in military activities. This approach recognizes the need for a plan to meet basic human and environmental needs, and the urgent requirement to shift national resources away from military-defined objectives to national needs such as industrial renewal, environmental restoration, sustainable economic development, social investment and renewable energies. Such a national needs policy, although initiated by government, should operate in partnership with industry, finance and local and regional authorities, workers and consumers.[56]

Conversion can help developing countries to escape the development trap by its immediate impact on the economy, the environment, and its reduction of high militarization levels. It can achieve its goals in a short time and at modest costs.[57] Converting conscripted labour is almost without cost because conscripts can return to their regular professions. Most conventional weapons can be disarmed fairly simply, and can be stored at very low cost. Many military land areas can be reclaimed for civilian use after minimal cleaning up. The extreme cases and obstacles to conversion do not apply to most developing countries as most do not have nuclear, biological or chemical weapons or well-developed arms industries.

Conversion provides huge potentials for environmental conservation, both by better use of resources for the development of a sustainable environment, as well as the clean-up of the environment already ruined by military activities. Conversion can also assist environmental conservation in the areas of environmental monitoring, chemical analysis, cartography, medicine, microbiology and radiology, besides the deployment of members of the armed forces for disaster relief and other emergencies.[58] However, transferring resources from military to civilian use will not automatically bring about environmental improvements unless such aims are built into the conversion process.

Conversion also provides an opportunity for economic development plans aimed at countering poverty. The reallocation of resources from military to civilian sectors should take place both domestically (within developing countries) and internationally.[59] Although there are a number of political, institutional, economic and technological problems associated with disarmament and adjusting to lower levels of military spending, not all of them apply to developing countries, and particularly Africa.[60] An important overall problem with conversion of defence industries, irrespective of the country involved, relates to the nature of the military industrial production process. This involves manufacture of a product for one major customer (usually the Ministry of Defence) which is based on 'a performance at any cost' principle, and has a product development culture which is determined by the inherently closed nature of military secrecy.[61] In Africa this is relevant only for Egypt, South Africa and Nigeria, where the military industrial base is well-developed. These form significant barriers of entry to, and exit from, the defence market. When added to the obvious adjustment costs at industry, company, regional and local community levels associated with restructuring or converting defence industries, they provide some of the reasons why very few countries have fully succeeded in converting defence industries to civil production.

Unemployment is usually cited as the real obstacle to reducing military spending and conversion. But this can be solved if the released resources are directed to productive civilian projects which create jobs, or other areas of public expenditure. Other barriers facing conversion include managerial reluctance to convert; the specific nature of the military product concept; the closed organizational culture surrounding military production; and the vested interests of the 'military industrial complex'.[62]

Nevertheless, the evidence suggests that developing countries *can* achieve reductions in military spending and implement conversion policies, and that this process of demilitarization has significant long-term economic benefits. This is true for most developing countries, and particularly African countries, because of the absence of military industries, which means that there are fewer economic and technological obstacles to conversion. What is needed is proper planning for conversion, and strategies for the use of military personnel and military facilities (such as airports) during peacetime in civilian projects.

Regional confidence building and cooperation among developing countries is also needed if military reduction and conversion policies are to become a reality. The developed countries must play an important role by making drastic reductions in arms trade, and supporting an international register of arms exports and production. In conclusion, reductions in military spending and the conversion of defence industries represent an economic opportunity rather than a problem.

4

Militarism, the UK Economy and Conversion Policies in the North

Steve Schofield

Today's militarism has historical roots. This chapter looks briefly at the historical background to militarism and its role in the UK economy. It focuses on the importance attached to technological capabilities as well as attempts to reorientate government industrial policy and research priorities from the military to the civil. It is this legacy that points to a paradox facing the UK at the end of the Cold War. Despite some demilitarization of civil society, reflected in opinion polls which show defence as an issue of declining importance, an elite military/industrial network of defence planners, politicians and industrial interests continues to exert considerable influence over important resources of technological expertise and capabilities – to the detriment of the UK economy.

Only by recognizing the continuity of militarism as an important influence on industry and technology can we begin to appreciate the significance of the end of the Cold War. For a large proportion of the population it represents the opportunity for a peace dividend and the transfer of resources from defence to the pressing needs of the civil economy, public infrastructure, education and the welfare state. For a military/industrial elite, however, it represents nothing more than a period of retrenchment in an attempt to ensure that cuts are kept to a minimum. As a result, military preparations will continue to make excessive demands on scarce industrial and technological resources and the UK will make no real contribution to disarmament and common security, despite the unprecedented opportunity offered by the end of the Cold War. On the contrary, the UK represents a major force in the new militarism underpinning the new world order.

Change is possible, however, through adoption of conversion policies. The second part of the chapter looks at conversion policy in the US and former USSR, assesses the potential for similar policies in the UK and EC and suggests what a comprehensive conversion policy should include.

WHAT IS MILITARISM?

Defining militarism is not an easy task. One definition confines the term to those sorts of ideologies which actively glorify warfare, for example fascism. War *preparation* which does not actively promote war itself is not, in these terms, militarist.[1] Militarism, though, can be related to all industrial society when defined as an excessive reliance on war preparation involving social, economic, political and ideological mobilization. Some argue that in Western liberal democracies a policy of defence and deterrence does not constitute militarism because it is a legitimate and realistic stance in a world of competing nation states, and, during the Cold War, between competing superpowers and their allies. However, while militarism has shed the overt ideological or imperial baggage of the past, it still depends on the contemplation of, and preparation for, massive destruction through the use of military force.

A crucial issue here is the importance attached to the technology of war in advanced industrial societies. Smaller armed forces have a range of sophisticated equipment such as fighter aircraft and missiles at their disposal which gives them increased capabilities compared to the much larger armies of the past. Therefore, it is entirely possible to have increased war preparation (including nuclear weapons) since 1945, but to see demilitarization take place in civil society.[2] This distinction is extremely important for our analysis. Essentially, the militarization of government industrial and technology policy can be contrasted with the partial demilitarization of society. As defence and military concepts of security decline in importance for civil society it should be possible to raise the profile of common security with its emphasis on environmental and developmental priorities, coupled to a programme of arms conversion with which to maximize the potential for the release of resources from the military to the pressing needs of civil economic reconstruction.

TECHNOLOGICAL MILITARISM

The idea that, historically, UK government policy can be characterized by a commitment to this form of technological militarism is a highly controversial one. The common perception remains that establishment culture was anti-industrial. Successive governments showed disdain for the northern metropolitan industrial bourgeoisie as opposed to support for a southern, finance-dominated, land-owning aristocracy; this was reflected in the composition and orientation of the British civil service. The most well-known illustration of this argument is that the UK was unprepared for conflict in the 1930s, especially in comparison to the fascist war machine.[3]

Recent work has questioned both this specific case and the underlying assumption of anti-industrialism. There is powerful evidence that government, in partnership with key industries, had a clear strategy for industrial and technological capabilities with which to wage modern warfare. Production figures show a sustained growth throughout the 1930s, especially in aircraft production:

> The RAF, centred on Bomber Command, its huge industrial base employing over one and a half million people, and its massive numbers of largely non-combatant personnel, some one million, represented a technological way of warfare.... Contrary to myth, the average English serviceman had at his disposal a much greater quantity of material than did his German enemy, or his Soviet ally, though less than his American cousin.[4]

Set against the staple diet of post-war films, which concentrate on epic struggles like the Battle of Britain with all its imagery of individual heroism, the reality was technological warfare through massive offensive bombing against civilian targets. As Edgerton says:

> To think of the English state as incapable of planning, of investing in science and technology, or of appreciating scientists and engineers is to misunderstand it and to absolve it from the responsibility for its actions.[5]

This commitment to war preparation has been an enduring feature of post-war UK policy, despite the initial run-down of defence spending at the end the Second World War and the successful conversion back to civil production. After falling to one-seventh of its wartime peak in the late 1940s, the onset of the Cold War, signalled by the beginning of hostilities in Korea in 1950, saw the Labour government expand defence spending from 6.5 per cent to 10 per cent of GDP. In fact, the Attlee government planned to double defence expenditure, including a fourfold increase in defence equipment production. This proved impossible to implement because of the strain on government financing.[6]

For the first time in history, the Cold War created a permanent peace-time military-industrial capability at sustained high levels of defence spending. Even Marshall Aid, which had been instrumental in establishing European recovery, was transformed by the US from aid for civil reconstruction to aid for rearmament, before being wound down altogether.[7]

In summary, the UK has maintained a range of commitments far in excess of what one could consider normal for a medium-sized European country, despite the reduction in its global status since World War Two. These commitments include strategic nuclear forces and conventional defence of Europe, the Atlantic, the English Channel and the direct defence of the UK (including overseas commitments like the Falklands).

Since the late 1960s, half of government expenditure on research and development (R&D) and between 20–30 per cent of total national spending has gone on the military. Even allowing for statistical uncertainties, this represents a heavy burden. Apart from the US and the former Soviet Union, UK government spending is matched only by France, although the US dominates military R&D spending in absolute terms.[8] Equipment demands to satisfy these commitments have been met mainly from UK defence companies and the Ministry of Defence (MoD) is British industries' biggest single customer. Continued spending on each new generation of highly sophisticated and specialized weapons systems across the range of requirements has meant that R&D consistently absorbed up to 20 per cent of annual procurement expenditure during the post-war era.[9]

DEFENCE SPENDING AND THE ECONOMY

Does this all matter? Would the UK, in economic terms, have been better or worse off without rearmament? A brief historical review reveals very different interpretations. For classical economists including Smith and Ricardo, the issue was very clear cut: military preparations were always a burden:

Taxes which are levied on a country for the purpose of supporting war... and are chiefly devoted to the support of unproductive labourers, are taken from the productive industry of the country. When, for the expense of a year's war, twenty millions are raised by means of a loan, it is twenty millions which are withdrawn from the productive capital of the nation.[10]

In 1841, Sir Robert Peel also strongly endorsed this view of the economic impact of military preparation and the need for disarmament:

Is not the time come when the powerful countries of Europe should reduce those military armaments which they have so sedulously raised?...The consequence of this state of things must be that no increase of relative strength will accrue to any one power, but there must be universal consumption of the resources of every country in military preparations.[11]

However, the recent experience of the Second World War stood this argument on its head. For many, the demands of military production seemed to bring an end to the mass unemployment of the 1930s. One of the rationales in the US for the inevitably large military expenditures of the Cold War was that government support for military procurement, particularly high technology equipment, would be the dynamo of a successful economy – what has become known as *military Keynesianism*. Indeed, the foreign policy documents which put forward the rationale for the US's new global military presence included a specific element on the benefits to the economy.[12] The Administration's Bureau of Budget, however, argued that far from being beneficial, these expenditures may result in substantial difficulties for the economy:

security rests in economic as well as military strength, and due consideration should be given to the tendency for military expenditure to reduce the potential rate of growth, and at an advanced stage to require measures which may seriously impair the functioning of the system.[13]

The body of literature on the damaging effects of military spending has grown, with Chalmers' work in the UK and Melman's in the US being most prominent.[14] In the UK, for example, the high level of military spending lowered the potential for investment in the overall economy which, in turn, contributed to the relatively poor post-war economic performance.[15] Labour's National Plan of 1965 neatly reflected the dilemma posed by high defence spending: 'If we endeavour to support too large a defence effort, it will create economic weakness which will, in the long run, frustrate our external policy as a whole no less than our internal policy.'[16]

UK GOVERNMENTS AND TECHNOLOGY POLICY

The first Wilson government in the 1960s stands out for its remarkable and ambitious challenge to the military orientation of science and technology in the UK. Wilson's overriding policy goal was to modernize British industry – producing a new Britain forged in the 'white heat' of the technological revolution. Subsequently the term fell into disrepute, as part of the general perception of failure surrounding Wilson's first administration. But a recent re-evaluation suggests that behind the imagery not only was there a clear and coherent analysis of the failings of the UK in its concentration on defence and other prestige projects, but also a recognition of the need for a radical overhaul of government institutions to maximize the potential for technology transfer into key civil areas, namely machine tools, electronics and telecommunications. The 'white heat', therefore, can be seen as forging a new, dynamic *civil* economy in response to the long-term imbalance in British science and technology towards the military. As Tony Benn, the Minister for Technology at *Mintech* (as the department became known) said:

> Having inherited the finest complex of research facilities available anywhere in the Western world, it has been my object to bring about a shift from the almost exclusive concentration of government support on defence research to more general support for civil industry.... There is no reason why in education or some other similar field of civil expenditure there should not be similar stimulation by means of public procurement in technologies associated with areas other than defence.[17]

Initially, Mintech had responsibility for a range of research facilities including the National Research Development Corporation and the Atomic Energy Authority, which included very large establishments like Harwell and the Atomic Weapons Research Establishment, Aldermaston. In 1967 Mintech also took over the Ministry of Aviation, which included the Royal Radar Establishment (RRE), the largest electronics research centre in the country, and the Royal Aircraft Establishment. As the Ministry of Aviation had also been responsible for a large proportion of the defence procurement budget, Mintech could then be accurately called a super ministry, in charge of all civil industrial policy and the bulk of defence R&D and procurement.[18]

Mintech set about promoting technology transfer. Examples include the biomedical technology work at Aldermaston: research into the materials and design for surgical implants, components for kidney dialysis machinery, patient monitoring systems, and so on. Most publicity was given to the work on artificial limbs. The RRE did pioneering work on infra-red systems for use in monitoring processes and quality in smelting metals, particularly steel and aluminium, plastics and ceramics.[19] The difficulties with technology transfer from defence R&D should not be underestimated, however. These include the different demands of civil markets, the tendency to over-engineer to solve problems without adequate appreciation of cost implications, and scepticism from industry on the merits of the exercise. Nonetheless, progress was clearly made over a very short timescale. However, after Labour lost the election in 1970, Mintech was split into various departments. The research establishments were taken into the Ministry of Defence Procurement Executive and the experiment in technology transfer effectively dropped.

Since 1970, very little has changed in the military orientation of R&D under succeeding Labour and Conservative administrations. Given the astonishing transformation in European security since the end of the Cold War, major cuts in defence spending and a renewed interest in the sorts of policies pursued under the Wilson government might have been expected. However, the gradual decline in defence spending since the peak years of 1985–86 has brought it back in real terms only to the level in 1979 – Cold War defence spending for a post-Cold War environment.

Two aspects need stressing about the historical continuity of UK militarism. First, the end of the Cold War was not seen as a signal for the fundamental re-evaluation of defence preparation and defence spending. In fact, the government's defence review in 1990, *Options for Change*, reflects the emphasis on technology, reassuring its readers that the numerical reductions in forces will be counterbalanced by improvements in equipment. The UK will play a leading role in NATO's Rapid Reaction Corps which is intended to provide for high-intensity operations around the world. In other words, military capabilities, particularly through improved technology, will remain a high priority, inevitably reflected in defence expenditure.[20]

Also, unlike the first Wilson administration, the Conservative government sees no opportunity to re-orientate priorities for technology policy. This is graphically demonstrated in the establishment of the Office of Science and Technology (OST) under William Waldegrave in 1992. Its remit is to coordinate the science and technology programmes of government in order to provide a clear strategic direction which, in turn, should improve industry's potential to benefit from the UK's undoubted capability for innovation. OST, however, will only be responsible for just over a fifth of the budget allocated for science and technology. Most obviously, the MoD, which still consumes 44 per cent of the government's total R&D spend, remains separate. Although there is a nominal commitment to working with the OST and liaising with other government departments, the MoD sees its main responsibility to be the procurement of weapons. Any strategic contribution to government science and technology policy is rejected.[21] Despite some modest programmes of access to industry there remains a 'ring fence' around the MoD.

The contrast between the Wilson experiment and the present situation could not be clearer. As a pioneering venture, the crucial importance of Mintech in the 1960s lay in its attempts to redirect state support for R&D away from the defence sector to technologies directly needed for the modernization of the UK's civil manufacturing base on the basis of a clear and unambiguous government strategy. In contrast, Conservative policy rejects both the prospects for a substantial peace dividend and the concept of a radical re-orientation of technological priorities despite the clear need for a similar strategy of modernization in the 1990s.

ARMS CONVERSION POLICIES

Today, there is no shortage of research on the positive economic benefits of reduced defence expenditure and arms conversion. The most recent is the IMF's analysis which suggests that international trade would benefit from an internationally coordinated decrease in defence spending of 20 per cent. This is significant not only for the major defence spenders in the West but for developing countries with large military budgets that would experience a growth in tradeable consumer goods.[22] Although conversion in the UK is not yet on the government's political agenda, it is an element of policy in the former USSR and the US.

The former USSR and Russia

The most comprehensive policy for conversion was begun by the Gorbachev leadership in the former Soviet Union. Two elements are central to understanding its significance: first, the sheer scale of the cuts in defence expenditure (by 1993 defence production was at a quarter of 1988 levels and defence R&D was virtually at a standstill); and second, the importance attached to the defence industries as key industrial and technological assets which would make a major contribution to the overall programme for economic reconstruction.[23]

Under Gorbachev, the centralized planning structure was still intact and a top-down policy was implemented for conversion, with the various ministries responsible for implementing a national plan. Building on the experience in civil production, Gorbachev called for rapid progress to help overcome the major shortages in consumer goods. Joint ventures with Western companies were also encouraged, partly to gain assistance in technology and commercial business practice but also as a way of linkage between conversion and broader security objectives:

> What is emerging in the Soviet Union is an official policy which closely links the issues of security and international cooperation in conversion. Extensive foreign involvement in conversion and the development of large-scale international projects involving the Soviet defence industry are seen as means of enhancing confidence in the irreversibility of the disarmament process.... The hope is clearly that such international cooperation will facilitate further demilitarisation of the Soviet economy and possibly also that it will make it more difficult for any conservative forces to put the process of reform into reverse.[24]

It is generally agreed that the expectations for the economic benefits from conversion were far too high, particularly in the short time-scale envisaged by Gorbachev. Much wastage occurred because of concentration on the capabilities of defence industries rather than the needs of the markets for commercial goods and because of duplication of production across defence establishments. Nevertheless, the commitment to radical restructuring and sustained cuts in defence spending remained up to the time of the collapse of the Soviet Union.

If anything, the speed of the cutbacks under Yeltsin in Russia was even greater than under Gorbachev with the demilitarization of the economy remaining a crucial element of the new administration's policy. However, tension developed between the supporters of privatization and conservative forces in the administration and the defence industries, who saw the latter's technological capacity as threatened. Even so, the scale of change is impressive, with 778 establishments undergoing conversion, 347 research organizations and an overall target of 900 establishments by 1993. A survey of 600 enterprises suggested that the share of military output had declined from 51 per cent in 1990 to 41 per cent in 1991 and was forecast to be only 26 per cent by the end of 1992. Over 877,000 workers left military work, with 536,000 re-hired on civil work at the same enterprises and 340,000 left unemployed.[25]

By 1993, there was clearly a power struggle between conservatives centred around the defence industries and those supporting privatization and conversion. While radical privatization was still the official policy there was an emerging debate about the retention of a state-owned defence-industrial base and private or joint-ownership of industry to provide diversified civil and defence manufacturing groups.

These structural changes to conversion policy since Gorbachev reflect broader policy debates on the transition to a market economy, the scale and speed of change, and in particular, as far as the defence industries are concerned, the continued role of the state in areas of strategic importance. As the defence industry has been run down, conservative forces have, unsurprisingly, rallied round the concept of a defence-industrial base and the retention of state ownership in order to protect themselves. Clearly, at a time of considerable economic disruption, there is a real danger that these forces could instigate a re-militarization of the economy.[26]

Nevertheless, considerable efforts have been made to sustain the momentum of reductions in defence expenditure and conversion despite the overarching problems of transition to some form of market economy. In the absence of financial support from central government it is not surprising to see new organizational structures emerging, including increased emphasis on city, regional and republic conversions programmes.[27] Perhaps the future for conversion lies, on the one hand, in this greater emphasis on local initiatives and, on the other, in support from the West through financial aid, management and industrial expertise and so on, as part of what should be a comprehensive programme of assistance by Western governments.

The US

During the 1992 presidential election campaign, Bill Clinton stated clearly that he saw the end of the Cold War as an opportunity for the US to refocus on international economic rather than military challenges into the next century: 'I know the world's finest makers of swords can and will be the world's finest makers of plowshares,'[28] he said, advocating an arms conversion policy as an important element of the broader strategy to help restore America's international competitiveness in civil markets. The policy would focus on retraining, technology transfer, R&D and community assistance with federal agencies taking a pro-active role in encouraging private sector initiatives.

During the election, he had called for cuts of $60 billion in defence spending over five years. Although only a relatively modest cut in real terms, leaving the budget at $274 billion in fiscal year 1993 – around 95 per cent of the Bush administration's planned spending – it would still have a considerable employment and economic impact. According to the National Commission for Economic Conversion and Disarmament, those facing redundancy included 290,000 military personnel and Department of Defence (DoD) and Department of Energy (DoE) civilian staff; 75,000–100,000 civilian defence workers and 250,000 others because of the lost spending power of defence workers.[29]

A variety of federal departments and programmes will be used to compensate for reductions in defence spending by investment in new infrastructure and high technology. The Advanced Research Projects Agency (ARPA), which has dropped Defence from its title in recognition of the changed emphasis, has a $400 million budget to encourage defence companies to adopt dual-use technologies which have applications in the civil as well as the military sector. However, ARPA's primary responsibility remains as a defence agency to meet military needs.[30]

Allied to stimulation of dual-use capabilities is a policy to re-orientate R&D from military to civil work. This includes the largest government R&D institutions such as the nuclear weapons laboratories Lawrence Livermore, Los Alamos and Sandia. These laboratories face considerable reductions in nuclear work, although various activities in weapons' safety and environmental clean-up will continue. The laboratories also have an extensive range of capabilities which can be applied to civil research. Some question how effective the laboratories can be in responding to new challenges and the need to streamline bureaucratic procedures for commercial work. They argue that the laboratories should be run down and new institutions given the responsibility for civil research.[31]

The Office of Technology Assessment (OTA) has outlined how the federal government can provide a clear strategic lead through new national programmes in areas like pollution-free transportation systems and fuel-efficient cars. Such a 'national needs' agenda would create a new vision for science and technology policy that would galvanize the research establishments in a way that only defence research could do in the past. However, defence R&D, despite its reduction to a target of 50 per cent of federal R&D, will still retain a major role and doubt must exist as to the scale of the restructuring that can be achieved.

Support to the Office of Economic Adjustment (OEA) in the Pentagon, in existence since the early 1960s to assist communities faced with base closures, has also been increased. Finally, there is an extensive programme of assistance mainly for military personnel and DoD/DoE civilians through early retirement, job retraining and so on.[32]

The role of state administrations acting independently of federal government is another important element of conversion policy in the US. For example, Connecticut, which is the most dependent of all states on private defence industries, has a package of financial aid including loans and investments in new product development. This is mainly targeted at smaller industries but a grant of $1 million was also provided to the Electric Boat Company, builders of the Trident submarine.[33] In California, an organization called Calstart made up of 40 public and private bodies is investigating options for using the state's aerospace expertise in new urban transport systems.[34] Many other examples could be cited, suggesting that, as the pace of defence restructuring accelerates, the role of the states and regional initiatives will be of increasing importance.

There are two broad interpretations of the significance of the Clinton conversion policy. One sees it as too little in the context of major restructuring at the end of the Cold War and, therefore, a missed opportunity. The other, despite defence spending remaining at historically high levels, sees the Clinton administration as having put together a comprehensive and realistic programme which, although modest, recognizes the major cultural changes that have to take place in the defence sector. These changes cannot be achieved overnight.

Despite concerns over the relatively small scale of resources and the emphasis on dual-use technology, the administration has addressed many of the areas that conversion advocates stress are vital in creating a positive institutional relationship between government and industry. Above all, the Clinton administration has tried to stimulate a political climate that is conducive to conversion. It treats conversion as a serious element of an overall economic and industrial policy that aims to raise the technological capabilities of US industry at a time of intense international competition. A new national agenda for civil R&D is a significant element of this effort.

However, the federal structure is not comprehensive and state initiatives are still peripheral given national policies stressing the maintenance of a defence-industrial base and dual-use capabilities within a large military budget. Generous assistance to retraining and other programmes for defence personnel may actually be counter-productive if it reinforces a pattern of consolidation around defence contracting. Sustained, deep cuts in defence expenditure remain the most important prerequisite for a comprehensive conversion policy.

The UK and Europe

The Conservative government in the UK has an explicit policy of leaving defence restructuring to market forces. In practice, this has resulted in significant reductions in employment and industrial capacity. Cuts in employment were actually *larger* in proportional terms than overall defence procurement reductions as companies anticipated deeper cuts in the future.[35]

Some defence companies have achieved notable successes through diversification into civil production (while retaining their defence work). Examples are Dowty Aerospace in producing landing gear for Airbus and a GEC-Marconi subsidiary which successfully moved into the production of TV satellite dishes. But the general trend has been one of rapid rationalization with the prime contractors running down and closing large sites.

Recently industry itself has called for government to take a more proactive position. They fear that reductions in defence expenditure could seriously jeopardize the UK's position in leading sectors such as aerospace and electronics. For example, several industrialists from the defence sector argued in their evidence to the House of Commons Select Committee on Trade and Industry that government should develop a long-term strategy for technology acquisition across government departments with increased support in areas like R&D to maintain the UK's capabilities in key industrial sectors.[36] Lord Weinstock, the Chief Executive of GEC, also endorsed the setting up of a Defence Diversification Agency. This has been official Labour Party policy for many years, re-affirmed in the 1992 election manifesto, with the aim of assisting defence companies.[37]

In the absence of any central government policy, local authorities have been the focal point for conversion activity in the UK. These have been mainly local studies of defence dependency but in some cases there has been practical help through EC funding. In contrast to the UK, the EC has seen the run down of defence industries and the impact on employment as a serious problem on a European scale and one requiring support from EC structural funds, in much the same way that basic industries such as coal and steel have been supported in the past. The first programme of EC support, called Perifra, was established in 1991 to assist defence-dependent areas hit by major job losses. Local authorities in north west England, for example, received a one million ECU grant for a technology centre in Preston to provide a focus for local innovation as some compensation, albeit very modest, for the closure of British Aerospace's military aircraft factory there, while the Wirral authority's successful bid for funds was used to set up an employment advice centre for redundant workers from the Cammell Laird shipyard, which had closed due to the run down of defence work.[38]

The EC has recently initiated the more ambitious Konver programme to assist regions with problems of defence adjustment. The budget is made up of 85 million ECU from the European Regional Development Fund and 45 million ECU from the European Social Fund. Bids have been invited from local authorities and the UK has been allocated about £15 million, to be matched by private funding. The level of funding still remains modest but there are clear similarities with programmes run by the OEA and the state authorities in the US, and scope exists for future development.[39]

Overall, though, the scale of cuts in European defence spending remains modest despite the wide variations across countries. In general, European governments have left adjustment to industries themselves, resulting in large job losses, declining industrial capacity and very limited compensation through company-led diversification, although there are national variations with German companies such as Deutsche Aerospace (Dasa) having made strenuous efforts to reduce their level of defence dependency. Opposition parties like the Labour Party in the UK and the SPD in Germany have called for greater assistance, and, with the Konver programme now underway, debate on a European conversion policy is likely to intensify.

To some extent industry itself is beginning to respond with requests for greater government assistance but the scale of continued defence procurement is a major motivation to consolidation around defence work.

A comprehensive conversion policy

The critical element for comprehensive conversion, and one generally ignored, is a clear relationship between disarmament and economic policy. Conversion is not simply a technical exercise but one that fundamentally links new concepts of common security, stressing environmental and developmental priorities, to the irreversibility of transition from military to civil economy.

Governments, using the peace dividend, could give a clear lead through a new national agenda for civil investment and R&D in areas like environmental protection and infrastructure investment. Not only would this stimulate economic development, it would also give a clear political signal that conversion should be a significant element of policy. A clear *political* objective should be for defence industries to reduce their level of defence dependency and, in the longer term, to normalize industrial structure so that, instead of a permanent specialized defence industrial base, we have predominantly civil industries that also supply the declining need for defence equipment. In other words, the end of the Cold War should be treated as the end of every other major conflict in the past whereby the traditional industrial structure is restored.

A crucial element is the reorientation from military to civil R&D, which requires research laboratories to enter into new civil contracts with private industry. All countries such as the US, UK and France with large military R&D outlays need to consider the range of programmes necessary for moving to civil R&D, linked again to support for qualitative disarmament that will reign in the technological arms race.

Regional initiatives to help defence-dependent communities are also required so that, as with the successful examples of the OEA in the US, local economies can create a diversified and stable economic base. Assistance to defence companies would also be crucial in the transitionary phase between defence contracting with all its attendant requirements and the different needs of the civil sector. The expansion of public programmes would be a major stimulation in itself but further assistance specifically to defence industries would be required in R&D, product development and marketing in order to overcome the strong preference to continue with specialized defence contracting. A Defence Diversification Agency, as supported by the Labour Party, would be one way of providing institutional support but it would need clear powers to coordinate programmes between the Department of Trade and Industry (DTI) and the MoD.

A final element in a comprehensive conversion programme would be assistance to the East. Some joint agreements have been signed between western companies and former Soviet defence manufacturers and research establishments but they are still relatively few in number. Without western assistance, conversion could falter and pressure grow for a remilitarization of the economy.

CONCLUSION

The paradox of the UK's situation is the continuing process of demilitarization in civil society with expectations of a major peace dividend at the end of the Cold War, alongside the consolidation of a permanent peace-time war machine. Historically, there has been a long-term technological militarism with the aim of sustaining the UK at the forefront of military capabilities. Relative economic decline has been the consequence of this pattern of government expenditure.

At an international level, when comparing conversion policy in the East and in the West a further paradox is that the nearest to a model of comprehensive conversion, linking progress on disarmament to an irreversible programme of demilitarizing the economy, occurred in the Soviet Union at a time when the benefits were least likely to manifest themselves because of the overriding problems of transition to a market economy and the lack of support and assistance from the West.

In contrast, the West has carried out, in the main, only modest cuts in defence expenditure. Restructuring of the defence industries has been left to market forces in many countries like the UK, with the inevitable consequence of consolidation around defence work as the dominant pattern. While the Clinton administration's policies on conversion are a welcome contrast to the lack of support elsewhere, they are still relatively modest. It remains to be seen if they will form the basis of a more ambitious programme in the future but the overall trend in defence spending suggests only moderate cuts in comparison to the ones that could be made to the end of the century.

In this context, the stress laid on dual-use technologies needs to be carefully considered. If defence remains an important element of government spending, dual-use could reinforce rather than reduce the trends towards defence consolidation and bring increased demands on the civil sector to satisfy the needs of the specialized defence manufacturers. Only through a clearly articulated and implemented national policy of comprehensive conversion can we expect to see a normalization of production along traditional peacetime lines with predominantly civil manufacturing industry and research institutions providing what remains of the declining need for defence equipment. Demilitarization of the economy is as important for the 1990s as disarming the military.

5

Promoting Real Security – Implications for Policy in the North

Ben Jackson

The war on drugs in Bolivia, where peasant farmers grow coca, has multi-million US dollar backing and Britain's support.[1] It is, though, a losing battle. As one US official candidly explains: 'These people are not addicted to coca, they are addicted to food'.[2] The menacing portrayal of Third World drug growing is only one of the ways the western military represent the South as an increasing threat. In a world ever more divided between the haves and have-nots, the Soviet threat is being replaced by fear of those whose desperate demands for basic economic justice can only be contained by the gun. The fall of the Berlin Wall has not yet changed the old concepts of arms-based security.

However, drawing up the castle gates and arming ourselves against a 'chaotic and threatening' Third World will only fuel the cycle of war, repression and wasteful weapons spending blighting the lives of millions in the Third World. Policies must tackle the root causes of conflict and insecurity there:

- the desperation propelling peasant farmers to grow coca as prices for crops such as coffee cease to pay a living wage;
- the gross inequality and poverty upon which fundamentalism and totalitarianism feed;
- the insistence of the rich on maintaining their 'right' to cheap access to scarce natural resources.

Governments worldwide need to listen to what their citizens say makes them feel secure, in the dictionary's sense of being 'free from fear'. In wealthy countries people fear worsening crime, losing their job, polluted air and water. In the Third World poverty, illiteracy, landlessness and consequent powerlessness lead to daily insecurity for millions. Poor countries feel insecure in the face of the pressures of mounting debt, falling trade earnings and closed markets.

The World Development Movement (WDM) believes Britain and other Northern countries must shift the emphasis of their security policy and budget priorities to face these real threats. Britain, for example, cannot go on spending twice as much of its national wealth on the military as its European allies. It cannot continue to bear the long-term costs of excessive support for the military. This chapter argues that Britain should cut its military spending by half by the year 2000, bringing it down to two per cent of GNP. It shows how these savings could then be used to fund programmes for *real* security. It proposes a fundamental revision of Northern security policies, using Britain as an example, and a reordering of spending priorities to back up the real security agenda. Finally, it broadens the discussion to cover some of the issues facing Europe in responding to people's real security needs.

THE CHANGING WORLD

The British government's 1993 Defence White Paper *Defending Our Future* drew unanimous criticism from commentators for its failure, in the words of the *Financial Times*, to 'undertake a root-and-branch examination of Britain's defence commitments'.[3] A leading war studies professor, Lawrence Freedman, concluded: 'What we really need is a foreign policy review'.[4] For too long British security policy has been driven by the MoD, commented former Foreign Office Minister Tristan Garel-Jones. He argues that this 'military domination is an anachronism and must be curtailed: the decisions that have to be taken are essentially political.... Part of our strategic reassessment must surely lead us to the conclusion that military capability is only one of the instruments at our disposal'. Other instruments, he says, include 'national diplomatic effort, membership of international economic and security organizations, aid, overseas broadcasting and so on'.[5]

Such calls reflect the now urgent need for a rigorous re-assessment of:

• how Britain and other Northern countries seek to promote security;

- how much to spend on the military (and on what types of capability); and
- how much on other instruments of security policy.

This reassessment must reflect the policy realities of the new world: first, the ending of the Soviet threat; second, economic necessity; third, the increasing number of 'humanitarian interventions'; and finally, the continuation of conflicts.

After the Soviet threat

The first of these new realities is the ending of the Soviet threat, and with it the central assumption of Britain's military and security planning within NATO. Former enemies are now recipients of western aid and some are in the first stages of joining the European Union (EU). Several of these countries, including Russia, want to join NATO. Soviet military capability has been decimated by the end of the Warsaw Pact military alliance, the withdrawal of Russian troops from Eastern Europe, a halving in the former Soviet Union's military spending in 1992 alone[6] and deep cuts in conventional and strategic nuclear forces.

Despite these vast changes, British policy seems stuck in the Cold War era. Policy on the ground belies official statements of the 'irreversible transformation of the strategic setting'.[7] The British government sees military spending falling by only 12 per cent in real terms in the five years up to 1995–96 (not allowing for the costs of the Gulf War and redundancies).[8] Britain still keeps large army and air force deployments in Germany and has strongly resisted calls for major reform to Cold War institutions, notably NATO.

Economic necessity

With a growing public deficit, economic necessity adds weight to the urgency of reassessing Britain's high levels of military spending. Even so, despite accounting for nearly 10 per cent of total government spending, the MoD has been exempted from the government's major, long-term review of public spending announced in February 1993.[9] As scrutiny of spending in other departments tightens, so the pressure for greater MoD savings grows. Concerns about arms industry job losses are also being weighed against the evidence that Britain's economy has suffered, not gained, from heavy investment in the military. Britain spends nearly twice as much of its national wealth on the military than the average of its major European allies, 4.1 per cent compared to 2.3 per cent.[10] This is a hangover from the 1950s: the huge commitment in

1954 to station a large army and air force in Germany locked Britain into a pattern of devoting more of its national wealth to the defence of West Germany than any other country except the US.[11] However, Britain's brief post-war economic and political leadership of Europe has long gone, and the then devastated German economy is now the strongest in the continent. Yet the British Government is not grasping the end of the Cold War as the opportunity for a long-overdue rebalancing of military burden-sharing; instead it eagerly embraces costly new military roles such as leadership of NATO's new Rapid Reaction Corps. As the *Financial Times* has commented:

> Is there a case for economically battered Britain to outspend its richer European neighbours?... The motives behind such thinking too often stem from nostalgia for a country that was more powerful and relatively richer than it is today. More insidiously, attempts to keep up defence spending spring from a desire to impress the Americans and to maintain a place at top tables.[12]

Humanitarian intervention

Recent international crises have mixed up 'Third World development' and 'military strategy' as never before. Controversial 'humanitarian military intervention' in Iraqi Kurdistan, Bosnia, Somalia and elsewhere, poses many longer-term questions for development workers and military planners. A leading international relations academic, Fred Halliday, says it is 'arguably the greatest change to the international agenda in recent years'.[13] Many people's cherished beliefs in the sharp dividing lines between the 'non-political' nature of humanitarian relief and the – fundamentally political – use of force inside another country's borders have been hurriedly abandoned.

The initial enthusiasm for humanitarian intervention was prompted by the moral imperative of preventing tyrants from using 'national sovereignty' as an obstacle to the world community 'doing something' to bring help to needy peoples appearing on nightly broadcasts around the world. But 'short, sharp' military solutions have proved inadequate, with long-term questions raised about political status and how long to commit resources to safe havens. In Somalia,[14] ordinary Somalis and aid workers have come into the firing line of the troops supposedly there to help. Was the UN or the US in control? In Bosnia, was humanitarian intervention a fig leaf for the lack of early and more decisive western action? The soldiers themselves have complained that the politicians have failed to spell out a clear political purpose for their presence. Can, in fact, military forces do the job?[15] The answer is often no. A coherent, long-term strategy is needed to tackle the underlying political and economic causes of insecurity. Ensuring the hungry are fed and bringing peace are indeed inextricably linked. But developing the debate beyond the belated fire-fighting of humanitarian intervention is now crucial.

Continuing conflicts

Without a change of direction, the horrific body-count of conflicts will continue to mount. Despite the new and bloody hostilities in the former Eastern bloc, the greatest numbers of direct and indirect victims of conflict continue to be in the Third World – just as during the Cold War. The promise that, with the rusting away of the Iron Curtain, the superpowers could work together to douse wars in the Third World has been only partly realized.

The hurried retreat of the former Soviet Union from its Third World entanglements has helped resolve some conflicts, for example in the ending of the South African occupation of Namibia and its independence in 1990, and in allowing rebels to beat the formerly Soviet-backed Mengistu regime in Ethiopia in 1991. In Asia, the Soviets encouraged the Vietnamese withdrawal from Cambodia, and in the Middle East, western-backed North Yemen and the Soviet-backed South merged. In Central America, the easing of East–West tension helped bring progress towards the ending of a decade of civil war and brutal repression. But for every example of progress, there seems to be a counter-example of new or continuing conflict. According to the Stockholm International Peace Research Institute (SIPRI), the number of places in the world with at least one major conflict only dropped from 32 to 30 between 1989 and 1992[16] and most of these are in the Third World.

THE BRITISH RESPONSE TO THE CHANGING WORLD

There are two clashing strands of policy in Britain's response to this new world. On the one hand, the government has proclaimed a new determination to promote human rights, democracy and development around the world. British ministers were among the first to push the idea of promoting 'good government' in the Third World as an integral part of aid and development policies. Overseas Development Minister

Lynda Chalker spelled out some of the key components of the new approach:

> A major new thrust of our policy is to promote pluralistic systems which work for and respond to individuals in society.... We firmly believe that democratic reforms are necessary in many countries for broad-based sustainable development.[17]

Action to ensure 'respect for human rights and the rule of law' is also crucial. She says: 'We do not believe it is an interference in the internal affairs of sovereign states to raise human rights violations with them'. She has also said:

> The Gulf War has demonstrated how excessive military expenditure can create political and military insecurity. It can also seriously damage development by preempting resources. It is vital therefore for developing countries to examine their security needs and tailor their military expenditure accordingly. We regard an appropriate level of such expenditure as part of good government.

Yet these proclamations on good government are time and again brushed aside by recourse to a more familiar approach to 'solving' problems of insecurity in the Third World – military muscle. Where lucrative arms deals are to be had, human rights abuses are overlooked (as in Indonesia or in Iraq). Where dictators are deemed to be important for Britain's strategic interests, speaking out for democracy goes by the board, and military training and assistance is supplied (as in many Gulf states). This contradiction has intensified as the military in Britain and its allies seizes on conflict and insecurity in the Third World as a means to justify their large budgets, as outlined in Chapter 1. This 'threat from the South' thesis is most candidly expressed by US policymakers. In 1992, the Pentagon's first detailed planning exercise for the post-Cold War world was leaked to the press. Of the seven scenarios for potential foreign conflicts which could involve US troops over the next ten years, five centred on intervention in major regional conflicts in the Third World.[18] They included another Iraqi invasion of Kuwait; a coup in the Philippines; a 'narcoterrorist' coup against the government in Panama, threatening access to the Panama Canal; and a North Korean attack on South Korea.

The risk of losing the North's access to the South's raw materials is one major element behind these potential scenarios. The desire to protect access to the oil of Saudi Arabia and the other Gulf States leads to discrete, but clear, western backing for Iraq in its war against Iran.

This 'tilt' towards Iraq (in the words of one British minister at the time) was a key issue in the decision by the British Government to supply military-related equipment to Iraq in breach of its publicly-declared policy of arms restraint. Foreign Secretary Douglas Hurd recently underlined the resource issue when he warned of the 'new disorder' and of a 'chaos [that] would threaten our supplies of raw materials, our markets, our investments, our values'.[19] In *Military Intervention in the 1990s* (Routledge, 1992), the British Army's former Head of Defence Studies, Richard Connaughton, points to the 'growing, dangerous instability in large parts of the Third World' as the central rationale, arguing for military intervention as the 'new logic of war' for the 1990s.

The government's annual *Defence Estimates* have reflected this changing emphasis – British military strategy now places a much greater and more explicit stress on military action in the South outside the traditional NATO area. 'The old distinction between "in" and "out-of-area" is no longer relevant for defence planning', declares the *1993 Defence Estimates*. 'Instead the criteria will be the depth of British and allied interests involved and the implications for international peace and security', it adds. The armed forces will need a 'graduated range of military options, from the employment of small teams of Special Forces to the mounting of an operation requiring the deployment of a division with maritime and air support'.[20] Britain needs a 'national intervention capability' for potential military action around the globe, either acting alone or with other allies. However, while military capability on the ground is changing in response to the perceived threat from the South, in part this 'Third World threat' is just convenient ammunition to be used in spending battles with the Treasury. For example, Britain is putting up £3.56 billion as its share towards developing the Eurofighter 2000 – conceived in the Cold War as a response to the Soviet MiG-29. The Defence Minister Jonathan Aitken defends the project, saying, 'Russian aircraft are now being sold in increasingly worrying numbers to Iran and other Middle Eastern powers. Countries we regard as being hostile or unstable are acquiring Russian-built aircraft.'

Military training and the arms trade

Preparations for the direct use of force are just part of a wider range of more indirect military means deployed in the name of defending 'British interests'. Military assistance and arms sales are part of a pattern of support for Third World allies which is shrouded in secrecy. An extensive programme of military assistance to Third World countries (the precise list of recipients is secret) cost over £36 million in 1991–92, channelled roughly fifty-fifty through the MoD and the Foreign Office.[21] The MoD says its:

> military assistance takes place mainly in support of wider foreign policy aims; the defence objective is limited to promoting stability and military effectiveness in countries where we retain valuable facilities, including for transit and training, or where we have an obligation to assist in the event of a security threat.[22]

Military training has been given to dictators and military governments with scant respect for Lady Chalker's 'good government' indicators of human rights, democracy and development (including Indonesia, Somalia, Nigeria, Zaire, Sudan and Saudi Arabia). The government also works closely with the arms industry and its financiers to ensure that their activities mesh with official strategic and commercial goals. According to the *Defence Estimates*, Britain's arms exports are a 'key part of our wider diplomatic relationships with our friends and allies throughout the world'.[23]

Britain is the sixth largest arms exporter in the world – with 80 per cent of sales going to the Third World. It is also one of the permanent five members of the UN Security Council which account for 80 per cent of world arms sales.[24] In 1992, the government proclaimed a record £5 billion worth of new arms orders – a fifth of the world market.[25] The government actively supports selling arms around the world. The £10 million a year Defence Export Sales Organization (DESO), based within the MoD and with offices around the world, helps British companies to sell arms; as do the military attaches based in many British embassies. The government also promotes arms fairs, and, through the DTI's Export Credit Guarantee Department (ECGD), underwrites British companies doing business in countries regarded as credit risks. Over the last four years, a quarter of ECGD backing for export of major goods and projects has been for the military sector.[26]

Most major British banks are involved in financing the arms trade: Midland Bank, for example, established a special Defence Equipment Finance Team. During the House of Commons Trade and Industry Committee hearings into the Iraqi Supergun affair, Midland said how it 'appeared to us that the Ministry [of Defence] welcomed the team's activities'[27] and defended its involvement in lending to Iraq by stressing that 'ECGD must give specific approval of each particular transaction'.

Officially the government says it only encourages the sale of arms 'as long as this is compatible with our political, strategic and security interests and does not conflict with our international obligations'. Yet the government's promotion of the arms trade and the provision of military assistance is totally at odds with its espoused 'good government' policies on promoting regional security, human rights and development.

First, arms sales can increase violent repression and human rights abuses. Amnesty International has highlighted Britain's involvement in this 'repression trade',[28] including the export of:

- leg-irons banned by UN rules for the treatment of prisoners;
- an electronic torture chamber to the United Arab Emirates;
- tear gas canisters used by Chilean security forces; and
- telecommunications equipment for use in the notorious State Research Centre of Idi Amin's Uganda, where as many as 500,000 political killings took place.

The British Government repeatedly claims to 'take into account' the human rights record of countries to which it is exporting weapons, but refuses to give any details of the criteria involved. In reality, many of the top customers for British weapons are major human rights abusers and dictatorships.

Second, while rich countries are quick to chide the poor for diverting resources from pressing human needs to high military spending, they are slow to make the connection with the way they promote arms sales to these very same countries. For example, India and Pakistan between them are home to over a third of all the world's people living in absolute poverty – 460 million people.[29] Both countries are large recipients of British aid, and yet they are both major customers for British weapons. The Indian military has a budget 80 per cent larger than that for education and health; their Pakistani counterparts get twice what schools and hospitals do.[30]

Third, arms sales can fuel and prolong existing international conflicts or heighten the tensions that lead to war. In Somalia, the conflict has been fuelled by the large stocks of weapons left over from the alliances, first with the USSR and then with the US. Similarly in Afghanistan, there is a vast legacy of weaponry from the superpowers' previous activities. India and Pakistan seem on the brink of a third major conflict over the disputed region of Kashmir, with an intensified arms race between the two. Yet Britain supplies weapons to both countries. Indeed, India is second only to Saudi Arabia in the league table of British arms markets.

Ben Jackson

THE COSTS OF CONFLICT

As the earlier chapters have shown, the emphasis on military solutions to conflicts carries a terrible cost in human life and economic destruction. Efforts to defeat poverty and promote development will be doomed in many poor countries until conflict and the accumulation of weapons and military power are tackled.

The direct human suffering is clear, with children being among war's major victims. In the last decade more than one and a half million children have been killed in wars, more than four million disabled, more than five million have been forced into refugee camps and 12 million have lost their homes.[31] Worldwide many children have suffered torture, abuse, imprisonment and even recruitment as 'child soldiers'. Seventeen million people have had to flee their country as refugees from war and repression – a further 23 million are internally displaced.[32] The overwhelming majority of refugees are being hosted by other poor countries – over five million alone in Africa.

War's indirect casualties often far outnumber the victims of the violence itself. Most of the famines of recent history have been caused by, or are strongly linked to, conflict – Biafra, Bangladesh, Uganda, Ethiopia, Mozambique, Chad, Sudan, Liberia, Somalia. National economies are badly hit, infrastructure destroyed, food production drops, tax revenues fall and so on. Military spending swallows up wealth, inflation rises, panic and racketeering takes hold and currencies can plummet.

However, even before bullets are fired, they can kill. Total world military spending stands at an estimated $750 billion a year – the equivalent of the combined annual incomes of the poorest *half* of the world's people.[33] The Third World accounts for about 20 per cent of the global total of military spending – having grown rapidly from some 6 per cent in 1965.[34] The swift growth of Third World military budgets in the 1960s and 1970s[35] slowed and turned downward in the last decade as debt and falling oil and commodity prices squeezed economies – although average spending levels may now have levelled out once again.[36]

While poor countries' military spending may not be large in global cash terms, it still represents a heavy burden and competes directly with desperately-needed social spending within government budgets. Many poor countries in South Asia and sub-Saharan Africa now spend two or three times as much on arms as education or health. With the onset of a severe economic crisis in the 1980s the trade-off between the two became even more intense. The IMF itself recognized in an internal study 'the evidence that military spending tends to exhibit resilience under Fund-supported programmes that emphasise fiscal tightening'.[37]

A UNICEF/SIPRI study of the data for sub-Saharan Africa concluded that, although there are notable exceptions, high military spending as a share of national wealth tends to increase the child death rate.[38] But Ethiopia, until recently one of the most heavily militarized and poorest countries in the world, is moving the other way. Half a million soldiers have been demobilized. The military's share of government spending has fallen from nearly 60 per cent to under 30 per cent, while that on health and education has risen from 12 per cent in the late 1980s to nearly 20 per cent today.[39]

Military spending also distorts poor countries' economies over the long term and damages their prospects for economic growth by diverting investment, production and scarce trained personnel into the military sector. The flawed argument that military spending injects a boost into domestic industrial development holds even less water the poorer the country, as the poorest countries tend to rely the most heavily on arms imports. Scarce foreign exchange is thus squandered on arms, while military debt service now accounts for as much as a third of the total, according to the World Bank.[40]

THE ROOTS OF CONFLICT

The bleak cycle of poverty, conflict and environmental decay can only be ended when security strategies are redirected towards confronting their economic and political root causes. Governments have to tackle the glaring world inequalities and pressing unfulfilled needs upon which conflicts breed.

The causes of conflict, as we have seen in earlier chapters, cannot be reduced to one-dimensional formulas. Nevertheless, as SIPRI has concluded:

> Often internal security problems such as civil war or the loss of legitimacy of the government or even the state are directly attributable to economic crises, as in much of Africa. The central problem in the developing world is that of economic security.[41]

The failure of development to meet people's most basic aspirations leads to festering frustration and anger upon which some of the most bloody Third World civil conflicts feed.

In a number of open or simmering civil conflicts, the majority are kept from a fair share of the country's natural and economic wealth by a small minority (sometimes also ethnically distinct) who protect their interests by the threat of armed force. With growing pressure on diminishing natural resources, such conflicts may grow. The struggle for fairer access to land has been the basis for some of the most brutal and long-running Third World conflicts. In El Salvador, the peasant majority have been crowded onto the poorest, most ecologically vulnerable land, because two per cent of the population – the 'Fourteen Families' – controlled 60 per cent of the country. In Brazil in 1991, 54 people died in 383 land conflicts involving 242,000 people.[42]

The struggle over water is also a focus for conflict. For example, nearly 40 per cent of the groundwater Israel uses originates in the occupied territories, but it has denied permission to Arabs to drill for water; Jewish settlers consume four times per head the water that Arabs do.

Many of these cycles of civil conflict and underdevelopment have international dynamics – through financial and trade policies. Debt has been called the 'oxygen of the fire of war' by development writer Susan George.[43] This is shown in the immediate outpouring of anger at swingeing social cutbacks caused by debt packages, and in the remorseless desperation and hopelessness of the poor who are the main recruits of guerrilla armies across the world. The violence spawned by drugs growing shows how international economic pressures and local poverty combine to sow the seedbed of conflict.

The drug wars

Many peasant farmers growing coca in the Andean countries of Latin America are fleeing poverty, economic crisis and political violence. Inhabitants of the Chapare, Bolivia's main coca-growing region, came there fleeing poor land and low prices for their traditional crops – often under government and aid-backed schemes in the 1970s. Others were miners who lost their jobs when the international price of tin collapsed, and with it the Bolivian economy, in 1985. In 1993, a GATT report on Bolivia called on rich nations to cut their farm subsidies and open their markets as a way of supporting moves away from drug production. When the coffee price plummeted by half in 1989, the *International Herald Tribune* noted that the US 'had offered aid in the war against the cocaine dealers, but that aid is trivial compared to the enormous losses to which the international quarrel over coffee is subjecting them.'

An estimated one and half million people directly rely on growing coca in Bolivia, Colombia and Peru[44] – even though coca farmers only receive around 1 per cent of the final street value of cocaine. In Bolivia one in five of the economically active population is estimated to owe their income in some way to the cocaine trade, which is the country's biggest foreign exchange earner.[45] The cocaine trade has brought the Andean countries violence, corruption, growing numbers of young people addicted to the drug and environmental damage. But farmers go on growing because they have little other choice. As one Bolivian farmer said: 'Coca is the last resource we have. Foreigners come and tell us to grow different things but the soil has been spoilt by coca and we have no market or transport for other products.'[46]

Instead of addressing these economic causes of drug production, the importing countries, led by the US, have made coercion their main weapon. In 1989 President Bush announced a 'war on drugs', centering on the Andean Initiative, a five year $2.2 billion plan to curb cocaine production[47] – half of which was earmarked for military and police assistance.

Britain has been a strong supporter of the US approach.[48] British aid and Foreign Office funding has been supplied for drugs-related training and equipment for police and customs officials from Indonesia to the Caribbean. In 1989 John Major, as Foreign Secretary, promised to support the US strategy with a first tranche of what would be 'substantial' British aid in the form of training and technical assistance to Columbia in the war against drugs, which would 'draw on our experience of fighting terrorism'.[49] In 1990, the *Sunday Express* reported on the involvement of an SAS team 'under a cloak of secrecy' which had been sent to Colombia to 'pass on their skills to Colombia's internal security and intelligence agency'.[50] Colombian security forces have a prominent role in human rights abuses.[51]

The failure of the war on drugs illustrates that military answers offer no long-term solutions to the 'new' agenda of Third World 'security threats'. First, cocaine production has grown – as has consumption in both the US and Europe. A leaked Pentagon memo on US policy in January 1992 stated that the Andean Initiative had so far 'only marginally impacted on the narcotraffickers'.[52] Second, in a region just struggling to emerge into democracy and away from the dominance of the military in political life, it has bolstered the military. The presence of foreign troops involved in coercive measures against peasant growers threatens to build support for guerrilla movements. A US Congressional watchdog reported that US officials do not have 'sufficient oversight to provide assurances that the aid is being used as intended for counternarcotics purposes and is not being used primarily against insurgents or being used to abuse human rights'.[53]

Alternative approaches, tackling the problem at the roots, are possible. Britain does support international programmes to help put in place rural development schemes to give the poor an alternative to growing drugs. But such crop substitution programmes remain grotesquely underfunded in relation to the scale of the problem – and in comparison to international resources spent on fighting drugs-growing with weapons.

A BRITISH BUDGET FOR REAL SECURITY

WDM has argued for a shift in the emphasis of security policy to take account of all people's real security needs and the changing world. This recognizes:

- the end of the Soviet military threat and consequent need for NATO to scale down further its huge forces;
- the logic of reducing the disproportionate military burden Britain bears compared to its major European allies;
- the need to reject the growing thesis that 'threats from the Third World' provide a new rationale for not cutting forces;
- the potential for substantial long-term gains for jobs and economic growth to be reaped from reallocating military spending to other areas;
- the terrible human and economic costs of failing to tackle the poverty, global inequality, environmental pressures and militarization which constitute the most fundamental threats to global security.

Shifting the traditional emphasis on military power as the primary means by which governments claim to protect their citizens is a huge and multifaceted task. But it must be undertaken before the broken mould of East–West divisions hardens again along an even more damaging North–South line of confrontation. Policies to meet this challenge require a redirection of British military spending. Just how Britain could change its budget priorities in line with promoting 'real security' is set out below. To find the resources for such a shift means reducing the amount of national wealth spent on the military by half, to 2 per cent of

GNP, the average of Britain's major European partners, by the year 2000. This cut-back on military spending presents two major policy issues: first, the wider effects on the economy and jobs and, second, the military implications of where the cuts would fall.

The arms industry and jobs

Halving British military spending is achievable. In fact, such a reduction is small compared to Britain's post-Second World War reductions and is comparable with cutbacks after the Korean War – both successfully implemented. Nevertheless, against the background of recession the prospect of high-profile job losses has led some to argue that the public enthusiasm for reaping the peace dividend is turning to a fear of a 'peace penalty'. In 1992 there were 433,000 jobs in the armed forces (about two-thirds services, one third civilian) and an estimated 135,000 jobs directly dependent on MoD contracts in the arms industries.[54]

The potential impact on the industry cannot, however, be examined in isolation from the wider economic implications of reducing military spending. After reviewing historical studies and economic projections of the effects of arms spending on jobs, three Cambridge and London economists recently stated that:

> The almost unanimous conclusion of these [studies] is, despite the predilection of economists to see a cloud behind every silver lining, that in economic terms disarmament is an opportunity, not a problem.... There is no evidence that cuts in military spending in conjunction with sensible macro-economic policies would cause an increase in total unemployment.[55]

They predicted that cutting UK military spending by 50 per cent by the end of the decade – as recommended here – could, in fact, create half a million jobs and add 2 per cent to the economy's growth over the period. The central reason for this is that while military cuts would hit jobs in the arms industry, they would also allow government to spend in other sectors which create more jobs per pound (in turn allowing these people to spend and create further jobs). In their model, the economists assume money is redirected across the range of government spending. WDM's Budget for Real Security allocates half to domestic spending and half overseas. However, even the savings earmarked for promoting real security overseas would have major pay-backs for Britain.

There is a notion that aid is something spent 'over there' and therefore is a net loss to the British economy. The reality is very different. Over 70 per cent of Britain's country-to-country aid is tied to buying British goods and services – from Land Rovers to power stations. For every one pound Britain puts into aid through international agencies, it gets back one pound forty pence. Even if stricter rules on untying aid were implemented, Britain would still be likely to get a good share of the business generated; indeed it might well gain. Debt relief too would bring benefits. According to one estimate, Europe has lost between half and three-quarters of a million jobs, as debt-strapped countries have had to cut back savagely on their imports. Britain, still a trading nation with a traditionally strong presence in the Third World, has suffered particularly from this process.

While reduced military spending could be a major opportunity for British jobs and the economy overall, programmes would still be needed to cushion the immediate jobs fall-out. Arms-reliant industries would need help to switch to civil production and develop strategies to diversify away from reliance on government funding through arms contracts to a successful high-technology civilian sector.[56] In the US, such a strategy has become a major plank of government policy, with $1.3 billion being spent on arms industry conversion in 1993. Gene Sperling, deputy economics advisor to President Clinton, said the defence conversion programme was a 'major sea change in economic policy' and that:

> from soldiers to scientists, it is morally right and economically right that we seek to redirect the energies and talents of the people who were responsible for winning the Cold War to the new investments in the economy that we need for national economic security.[57]

In Britain, although the government actively intervenes to support arms contracts, it insists that any conversion to civilian production must be left to the market. Three trade union leaders representing workers in the industries affected stressed that they:

> welcome without reservation the moves to a safer world. However, the one million British people whose livelihoods depend on defence spending deserve better than to be dumped on a government scrapheap.... As a matter of urgency Britain needs to plan the inevitable forthcoming changes so they do not result in vastly increased unemployment and economic disarray.[58]

In 1993, the conference of the Transport and General Workers Union passed a motion calling for 'a reduction of defence spending in Britain to the average level of other Western European countries'. It argued for the establishment of a Defence Diversification Agency and for the government to help channel resources into regeneration of Britain's manufacturing base where the 'industries could be developed by industries currently making military equipment'.[59]

Domestically, then, an agenda of action for conversion is needed which might include the government setting up the following:[60]

- a Conversion Agency within the DTI as a centre of export advice for those seeking to demilitarize their industry;
- a low interest fund to finance conversion, retraining etc;
- redirecting the 44 per cent of the government research and development budget which goes on the military to key civilian areas of the future – micro-electronics, biotechnology, telecommunications, robotics, civil aviation, computers, software – areas in which our low-military-spending competitors like Japan and Germany so often outstrip us;
- tax incentives and the strategic use of the government's civilian procurement budget to support conversion.

These elements of a national strategy should be part of a wider European approach and could be linked with existing collaboration on major civilian high-technology development programmes. They also require action at a regional and local level in Europe.

Military implications

The second major argument advanced against such a cutback is that it would cause an unacceptable loss of British military capability. The identification of new military threats against which we must be armed, as these critics would argue, has already been discussed in some detail. The point here is not to advocate the details of a precise package of cuts but to show that it should and could be done, while still leaving Britain with modern, well-equipped armed forces on a par with our European allies. The cuts suggested would still leave ample resources to ensure Britain was able to fulfil the two core military objectives of defending British home territory and coastal waters; and playing a major part in overseas deployments within carefully worked out UN-controlled, or other non-partisan, forces when called upon – for example in peace-keeping.

The key areas to tackle in achieving a 50 per cent reduction are:

*   stopping the expansion of Britain's preparations to fight wars in the Third World and curtailing funding which increases militarization in the Third World;
*   cutting weapons systems and personnel not needed because of the end of the Cold War; and
*   winding down Britain's end-of-empire overseas deployments.

Not expanding Britain's military capability for Third World involvement would mean cancelling such things as major new projects for amphibious capabilities. The first criterion would also mean curtailing funding for promoting arms sales and militarization in the Third World, including the closure of DESO; ending ECGD credits for military equipment; halting military aid and training for Third World countries (at least until a full and open review is carried out); and cutting back on military-related anti-drugs programmes.

The second criterion would lead to a major reduction of army and air force deployments in Germany, the cancellation or scaling down of expensive equipment projects (such as the Eurofighter 2000 or Challenger 2 tank) and other measures such as:

*   further cutbacks on submarines allocated to the Eastern Atlantic;
*   scaling down the number of frigates to about 25 (from the 48 in 1990 and the 35 envisaged in the White Paper);
*   cutting RAF squadrons to 14 (from the 33 in 1992 and the 24 planned for 1995); and
*   reducing central support services and training in line with overall reductions in service personnel.[61]

The third criterion would include winding down involvement in Belize (where withdrawal has already been announced), Hong Kong (planned after 1997 when it reverts to China), and possible reductions in the Falklands if diplomatic negotiations could achieve the necessary assurances.

Investing in real security – the financial implications

Under these proposals Britain's military spending would fall at about 8.5 per cent a year to about £12 billion a year (in current prices) by 1999/2000 from the £22.7 billion planned for 1995/96.[62] This would generate total savings of £42 billion – representing £1000 of every British adult's tax over the period (rising from £50 a year in 1994/95 to £300 by the year 2000).

WDM's Budget for Real Security would see half these resources redirected into British efforts to promote real security around the world, and half into domestic spending. Each of these halves could then be split again to fund equally four programmes to:

1. achieve the UN aid target of 0.7 per cent of GNP by the end of the decade, with money concentrated on programmes to tackle poverty directly, rebuild after conflict and help the victims of war;
2. cancel the poorest countries' debts and fund initiatives to resolve conflicts through diplomacy and other peaceful means;
3. invest in a programme for shifting Britain's economy away from making arms to civilian production and jobs;
4. allocate funds towards other pressing needs at home in a time of constrained government budgets.

Aid

Earmarking a quarter of the savings from military spending cuts for aid would fulfil an international recommendation set out by the United Nations Development Programme (UNDP).[63] It identifies two broad areas which should have priority call on the resources released by defence cuts: 'the urgent social problems in many industrial nations, from homelessness to drug addiction, and the wide range of development needs in the Third World'. It would enable Britain to reach by the year 2000 the UN target of 0.7 per cent of GNP spent on aid. Current spending planned for 1994/95 is £1900 million which gives an aid/GNP ratio of approximately 0.30 per cent. Increasing aid to developing countries (excluding Eastern Europe and the former Soviet Union) by £500 million each year, starting in 1994/95, would allow for a budget of £4900 million (at current prices) by the year 1999/2000. This would enable Britain to show an aid/GNP ratio of 0.77 instead of the likely further decline in the ratio expected in the next few years. Britain would have then reached the target 30 years after it was adopted by the UN and more than 25 years after being accepted by the British government, but would still expect to have a ratio lower than Norway, Denmark, Sweden and the Netherlands.

Increasing Britain's overseas aid budget to the UN target would also remove fears expressed by the House of Commons Foreign Affairs

Committee that the country's bilateral aid programme will be squeezed to unacceptably low levels by the escalating demands of commitments to the EC's development cooperation programmes (set to rise by 35 per cent by 1995/96) and the rapidly escalating emergency relief budget, up fivefold from £34.7 million in 1987 to an estimated £171.7 million in 1992/93. Part of this money is represented by the nearly £9 million ODA has had to refund to the Ministry of Defence between 1988 and 1992 for 'providing humanitarian services' such as RAF airlifts, notably Operation Safe Haven for the Kurds in Northern Iraq. As the ODA itself notes, 'this money spent on saving lives now is at the expense of funds for development and improving people's lives in the future'.[64]

A fully funded ODA programme will not have to face this unacceptable dilemma. The increase in aid could thus be used to promote real security, first, by ensuring that Britain had enough emergency funds to react to disasters around the world – many of them conflict-related – without digging into long-term funds. Second, it would enable expansion of assistance for countries and communities suffering from the effects of conflict or just emerging from war. Rehabilitation programmes are vital if fragile peace deals are to last. Help in rebuilding infrastructure, mine clearance and refugee resettlement would be primary candidates for such aid.

Third, it would fund programmes to tackle long-term causes of insecurity. A key need would be to increase the level of aid funds going directly to tackle poverty. UNDP has set a modest target of spending a fifth of aid on providing basic needs (which it defines as primary health care, sanitation, nutrition, clean water, primary education and family planning). At present, Britain spends only an estimated 8.8 per cent of its bilateral aid on these basic needs. Reaching the target of one fifth by the year 2000 would mean that Britain could spend nearly a billion pounds on these pressing needs (ten times what it does at the moment). This would be enough, for example, to pay for the estimated costs of ridding the world of polio. A 'basic needs' aid package which Britain could fund by the end of the decade could, for example:[65]

- provide basic health care services to 500 million of the world's poorest people;
- bring safe, piped drinking water to 4000 Indian villages and 20 small towns;
- supply a programme of improvements to the living conditions of 8 million Indian slum dwellers.

Remaining aid funds could also be channelled into economic development and environmental initiatives to benefit the poorest. Britain could, for example, contribute £22 million to match the French contribution to the International Fund For Agricultural Development's (IFAD) second Special Programme for Africa with its proven track record in helping the poorest farmers grow food, especially in drought-affected and desert-prone countries. Britain would also be able to contribute funds towards programmes to put into action the Agenda 21 programme of action for sustainable development, agreed at the Rio Earth Summit.

Debt and diplomacy

The second tranche of funds released from military spending would go to non-aid initiatives for promoting real security worldwide. One third of this money (ie £3 billion) would be enough to write off about 80 per cent of the debts owed to Britain by the poorest countries, in a deal to enhance the Trinidad Terms debt relief initiative along lines already suggested by the government.[66] The rest of the money could then be used to strengthen Britain's ability to solve conflicts through diplomacy and other peaceful means.

While the German and French governments have each increased spending on their diplomatic services, the British Foreign Office is being squeezed.[67] This is at a time when there is an unprecedented upsurge in the demand for diplomatic efforts to resolve conflicts and to support UN peacekeeping operations. Between 1983 and 1988, Britain's average annual contribution to UN peacekeeping was £10.5 million but by 1992 it had grown to £93.5 million.[68] In April 1993, *The Times* reported that 'peace keeping is expected to cost Britain an estimated £200 million in the current financial year – more than one-third of the Foreign Office's running costs'. Peacekeeping costs may not continue to grow at that rate, but the current level is unsustainable without the additional funding for the Foreign Office that is possible under the Budget for Real Security. This would fit with the spirit of UN Secretary-General Boutros Boutros Ghali's call in his *Agenda for Peace* to shift the cost of funding UN peacekeeping efforts from foreign ministry budgets to defence budgets.

Real security at home

The remaining half of the savings could then be used, first, to pay for the investment needed to put in place a comprehensive programme of central and local government action to fund the transition away from a military-reliant economy – of the kind outlined in the agenda for conversion. This could leave a final quarter of the savings to fund programmes to meet important social needs – from health to homelessness – which would also contribute to efforts to help stimulate the economy and create jobs in the process. Extra resources for domestic spending would also help ease the way for cutting Britain's large public sector deficit.

LOOKING BEYOND BRITAIN

Redirecting current military spending into areas that improve real security for all people is a central but partial answer to securing a well-developed world. Another requirement is for a much more open, accessible and wide-ranging approach to security issues. In Britain, as the Scott Inquiry into arms to Iraq has shown, the first step to redress the policy contradictions arising in the post-Cold War world is to increase public information on and political accountability over the government's arms trade policy. Without change, Britain will go on bolstering the violent regimes and regional arms races killing people in the Third World – and from which ultimately, as Iraq shows, we cannot isolate ourselves. The government should make available a register of arms export licence applications – with the right of Parliament to inspect, debate and veto such applications (along the lines of a system in operation in the US) in the light of their implications for human rights, development and regional security.

In an increasingly interdependent and interconnected world – from financial and communication networks to commercial and trading institutions – a broader, less nationalistic and military-reliant approach to security is needed. Work to bring this about must start at the national level, but cannot end there. Strategies for change must match the high-level international coordination of policy shaped by key institutions, such as NATO, which remain deeply imbued with the orthodox assumptions about 'security'.

The ratification of the Treaty on European Union (the Maastricht Treaty) means that the EU could be one of the most important institutional arenas for this debate in the next few years. The cause of some of the most ferocious debate, the Treaty's provisions for a Common Foreign and Security Policy (CFSP), opens the door for significantly greater coordination of security policy at an EU level, including 'eventually, the framing of defence policy'.

The stated aims of the CFSP include:

* preserving peace and international security in accordance with the UN charter;
* promoting international cooperation; and
* consolidating respect for human rights.

The CFSP will be applied by 'establishing systematic cooperation between member states'. Full-blown 'joint action' is to be introduced 'gradually... where the member states have essential interests in common'. Much remains to be decided: the speed and degree to which EU member states will in practice move down the path of Europeanizing security policy; the approach and content of any emerging EU security policy; and how any changes will affect the South.

The tide of political opinion behind the most ardent proponents of European unity may have slackened off. But those wishing to influence the direction of security thinking would be foolish not to shift greater attention to the EU level. The present lack of clarity about policy directions must be grasped as an opportunity to mould them. This means greater debate amongst ngos, academics and campaigners across Europe in order to develop a strategy for influencing the decision makers.

One starting point for ensuring that promoting development is at the heart of an emergent common policy could be the Treaty's commitment to ensure the 'consistency of measures carried out under the CFSP with measures carried out by the Community in the context of external economic relations and development co-operation'. This consistency would have to have regard to the Union's commitment elsewhere in the Treaty to foster the 'lasting economic and social development of the developing countries, and most especially the most disadvantaged of them' and its backing to the 'campaign against poverty'. The challenge is to make the grand words match the policy reality.

Proposals for controls on the EU's trade in arms and dual-use equipment with the rest of the world (18 per cent of the world total) reflect the deep lack of clarity in practical policy due to the Treasury's uneasy compromise between member states on this issue. A clearer EU policy is now an urgent priority, not only because of the moves to a CFSP, but also because the Single Market presents the danger of arms producers in one member state exploiting the lack of internal barriers to export weapons out through the country with the weakest export controls.[69]

Dual-use goods (those with both military and civilian uses) were meant to have been dealt with under the Single Market provisions; but the details of the regulation have still to be settled. Within the Maastricht Treaty, the issue of a common European policy on arms export regulation is recognized – but fudged and postponed in reality. The broad framework for a policy does, however, exist in a European Council statement of June 1991 setting out seven criteria on arms exports. These included: respect for UN sanctions and other measures; respect for human rights in the importing country; internal tension and conflict in the country of destination; regional peace and stability; and the possibility of arms being diverted or re-exported from the country involved.

But the statement's broad principles need to be tightened up with detailed and objective criteria for control if they are to work and are not to be interpreted in the way most politically expedient for the exporter. Action at a European level must also go hand-in-hand with attempts to press for controls in other countries (such as present attempts to do so in the US) and through multilateral fora such as the UN.

6

Conclusion:
Prophets and Practitioners

Geoff Tansey and Paul Rogers

For 45 years, the attitudes and policies of the northern industrialized states were dominated by the ideological divide and military confrontation of the Cold War. Now that era is past and we have a rare opportunity to work towards the creation of a more just and peaceful world. Instead, all the signs are that we are heading for a bitterly divided, unstable and dangerous world. We are often, as Maria Elena suggested in her introduction, our own worst enemy – unable to recognize the opportunities open to us as we retreat into the false security presented by military power.

The prospect of a divided world is all too real. As we have seen, a combination of circumstances and trends is likely to lead to heightened instability and conflict. On present trends the current deep polarization of the world community into wealth and poverty, power and dispossession, is set to grow still deeper. Within 30 years, barely one-seventh of the world's population will control and use three-quarters of the wealth and resources. Yet this will be a world in the midst of quite fundamental environmental constraints as the global ecosystem fails to cope with expanding human activity.

In essence, any improvement in the well-being of the majority of humankind will have to be achieved through routes quite different from those which have failed us so far. Moreover, the greatest pressure for changes in our economic system will be on the ecologically profligate populations of the North. Yet all the signs are that the northern states will not allow their materially high standards of living to be threatened by the needs of the majority – they will simply try to maintain their position through force. This is essentially self-defeating, for we now live in a world which experiences one core legacy of the 45-year Cold War – gross militarization. This is a global phenomenon, and its very profitability has ensured that military power has proliferated across the world. Any attempt to impose a northern security hegemony on the world community may appear to work initially but will inevitably lead to a growing reaction from southern states and the growing global underclass.

In 30 years time, a world of more than eight billion people, in which the power resides principally with a billion or so people in the North – from North America through Europe to East Asia – will be a world with billions of educated but workless and impoverished people who *know* how the rich and powerful conduct themselves, and who see their own futures being mortgaged by the economic profligacy of the minority. As environmental constraints limit any escape through traditional notions of economic development, frustration will turn to desperation and desperation to violence. This differs only in degree from our present circumstances, where social unrest and the crime which so often follows is countered by stronger policing and mass imprisonment, denial of human rights and, all too often, repression of the dispossessed.

In the final analysis, though, militarization is self-defeating, since an inevitable consequence is ultimately to supply southern states and some in the global underclass with many and diverse instruments of potential redress. These are not just the Armalite rifle or Semtex of the late twentieth century, but the nerve gases, biological warfare agents and suitcase nuclear bombs of the early twenty-first century.

BEYOND FAILED IDEOLOGIES TO NEW VISIONS

The present world order is not working. It is failing to meet the challenges of the rich-poor divide, of environmental constraints and of militarism, which cannot solve the conflicts inherent in the other two. What makes the discussion of real security so important is its call to a new vision of how things could be. To values of sharing rather than selfishness, of equality rather than exploitation, of negotiation not warfare, of shared international rules of coexistence between nations and peoples, not control by the strongest. It raises fundamental questions about *whose* security – of the strongest or the weak or everyone?

The post-Cold War world, with all its uncertainties and problems, also provides a major opportunity to inject analysis and vision into public debate – for a public that is worried and dismayed that the promise left by the fall of the Berlin Wall and collapse of communism has not been fulfilled. A major reason why the hoped-for change has not occurred is because the real problems in the world were not, and are not, the East–West division but rich world/poor world divisions over the distribution and use of power and resources. Dealing with this will require more than a rampant free market ideology, pitting one against the other, which is all that seems to be on offer from politicians, with its view that people are rather nasty, operate only from self-interest and that this self-interest is the only motivation for progress.

Idealism is realism for our human future. To think that the North can close the gates around it and keep what it has is wishful thinking. Change linked to a new vision of security is needed in North–South relations if we are to live together on a peaceful planet.

There is massive scope for demilitarization and a renewal of all kinds of research into other forms of economy and technology if the brain power locked into the military can be liberated for the human good. Actual world military spending could be cut by four-fifths and still be at around 1 per cent of GNP which has been the rate for many countries for over 20 years.

Environmental issues pose the most difficult problems because of their timescale – it may take 10, 20 or more years to feel benefits from actions now, when politicians tend to think, if we are lucky, in five-year horizons. Many people are working on change, however. One challenge is to bring them together into a complete rethink of our security needs and the kinds of institutions and actions required to meet these needs.

VISION – AND PRIORITIES

The issue of recapturing security from the military and defining it across all its human dimensions is highlighted by Ben Jackson. Once such a point is made, however, it leads to new economic priorities, to different budget allocations, to new forms of power distribution. To really address the issue it helps to approach it from the point of view of the poor. In the dictionary, security is defined as a freedom from fear, as being untroubled by danger. Poverty at the household and individual level is all about security. Robert Chambers, a rural development specialist, points to five deprivation points in household security:[1]

1. Material poverty – a lack of access to assets such as land, shelter, cash.
2. Physical weakness – as poor households were often physically weak.
3. Vulnerability – with few buffers against contingencies so that any little problem could knock them into destitution.
4. Isolation – hard to get products or skills to market.
5. Powerlessness – victims of the powerful.

So many of these chime in with the problem of insecurity. Development – as Jackson and others argue – is about overcoming poverty, injustice and powerlessness. It is a quest for security and safety at local and national level. The poor do not know from day to day, season to season or year to year where the resources they need are coming from. There is a coherence between a broader definition of security and development.

We must start at the level of the poor in the South (and in the North) and work through a political agenda we can use in countries, both rich and poor, to promote real security. If we go along the present military line we 'blame the victim', where the poor are seen as a threat. This leads to xenophobia, fear of migrants and racism. The rationale for aid in the 1960s, in the Cold War, or the impetus for land reform in Korea and Taiwan was motivated by a fear of what poverty might breed and the challenge it might make to the political order.

The political problem in recasting security is to say loudly that the way we think of security at present – as the use of, or threat of, military might – does not address what makes for human security, what *really* makes people feel safe. This is not the same as saying free from danger, but is being able to live in societies that can deal with danger and conflicts fairly, without descent into violence, terror or repression.

Development is essential for world peace and requires an agenda that:

- rejects notions of military superiority as the main plank of security policies;
- promotes international rule of law – applicable to all, equally;
- provides support for non-military resolution of conflicts, especially in the South. This takes resources. Even where there is the political

will to solve problems, as in Cambodia and Angola, sufficient
resources to bring it about are not made available;
an agenda for demilitarization and disarmament with a reallocation
of resources to deal with poverty through economic and
environmental programmes that tackle the causes of poverty and
inequality.

Human needs

In this process, we need to rethink just what human needs are and how
they may be met – something that ties in with the concern for
powerlessness. Although most discussion on human needs sees food,
shelter, clothing and such like as basic needs, Manfred Max-Neef,[2]
director of the Development Alternatives Centre in Santiago, Chile, calls
these *satisfiers* of more fundamental human needs. He identifies nine
fundamental needs: subsistence, protection, affection, understanding,
participation, creation, recreation, identity and freedom. How these
fundamental needs are satisfied varies but the needs he identifies are
universal. Subsistence, for example, is satisfied by *being* healthy,
adaptable, *having* food, shelter and work, *doing* things such as feeding,
procreating and resting and *interacting* with the living environment and
social setting.

These fundamental needs form a dynamic system in which no single
need is more important than another or which necessarily has to be met
before another. They are not a hierarchy. They may be met
simultaneously, complement each other and be traded-off against each
other. However, if the minimal need for subsistence is not met, the other
needs may be blocked and a single intense drive to fulfil it is likely. This
can be true of other needs too; for example, a complete lack of affection
or loss of identity can lead people to extremes of self destruction.

How and with what we seek to fulfil these needs matters. Some can
be fulfilled in ways that violate or destroy others; for example, the need
for protection might be met by an arms race, a national security doctrine
or authoritarianism. These can impair the satisfaction of other needs
such as subsistence, affection, freedom, participation and identity. Other
pseudo-satisfiers only *appear* to satisfy; for example, formal democracy
may only appear to satisfy the need for participation. Some apparent
satisfiers of one need inhibit others. Paternalism, for example, may meet
the need for protection but inhibits satisfaction of the needs for
understanding, participation, freedom and identity. Some satisfiers
satisfy only one need, such as food programmes meeting the need for

subsistence while others have synergistic effects, satisfying one need and stimulating satisfaction in others at the same time. Self-managed production, for example, may satisfy the need for subsistence and stimulate satisfaction of needs for understanding, participation, creation, identity and freedom.

Successful development produces satisfiers for the various needs which have synergistic effects on others rather than inhibiting or violating them, as currently happens with the need for protection or security. This approach recognizes that we human beings are multi-faceted creatures that cannot be reduced to a single variable – such as maximizing economic well-being. This becomes apparent when people talk about what security means to them as individuals and households and citizens of a local community, national entity, regional grouping and one world. They draw in concerns about work, freedom from terror, repression, environmental destruction, about the need to be active in shaping their environment and participating in decisions and actions that shape their lives. It is the antithesis of the consumer culture, which defines people by what they can buy and assumes all needs are fulfilled through what they consume.

Recognizing the range of human needs also shows that in redefining security we must face the need to involve a range of areas. This changes the ideological, psychological, economic and social understanding of security. Increasing human understanding of ourselves and our drives, and how we project onto an 'enemy' the attributes in ourselves we cannot come to terms with, is essential, otherwise our attempts to achieve protection or security are doomed. For unless we each understand the way the powerful gain consent for militarism and repression by focusing our anger and hatred on an enemy – either within or without national or ethnic boundaries – attempts to achieve real security are much less likely to succeed.

Education, as the satisfier of our need for understanding, is a slow but essential process. It must draw on the range of thinking underway about how our economies work, our societies function to meet human needs as well as the myriad of attempts by ordinary people to do so through all kinds of local-level cooperation, community action, and resistance to top-down remedies imposed by the powerful.

Spelling out more clearly our visions for a more secure future for humankind is vital if the opportunity for change is not to be wasted. Elements of the vision are around but a new synthesis still has to be developed out of the mess that the collision between capitalism and communism has produced this century. What is clear is that attempts to deal with the conflicts inherent in such an enterprise by military means, by the use of armed power, will not produce a world in which human needs are met, but one in which they are violated and destroyed.

We have to try to draw together the insights coming from the various people's movements struggling to deal with development, environment and peace and other issues. Likewise the ideas of those in the academic community working in a wide range of disciplines. Another challenge is to engage with and move those in government and military structures towards a new vision of security and to redefine their roles. An essential element in this rethinking is to unpick the image of masculinity and femininity, making roles more flexible, so that what matters is what a person is, and can do, rather than their gender.

While we see the need for a broad new vision and radical changes across economies and societies, it must be grounded in the specific experiences of different people. We cannot do everything at once: it is too much for most of us to take in. In Britain, for example, for people born post-war, with no experience of military service and a sense that economic growth was their birthright, you can pick examples of where the system is failing, and show how they relate to the changes needed. This is what many ngos do. Specific images shock us. We react to things we can relate to. Particular examples can show a pattern of development and how it is systematic of the whole economic and military system.

ACTION

Our vision is both demonstrated by our actions and developed through them. Putting the poor and the dispossessed at the centre of security and development means promoting specific actions that contribute to meeting the human need for protection and which also enhance our chances of meeting our other human needs. The actions needed to promote a peaceful world are legion. They run across boundaries – national and disciplinary. In deciding upon actions, however, it is essential to ask the right questions.

One question concerns the links between the North's policies and the South's willingness to demilitarize. Northern military strategies, as we have seen, are increasingly looking South for enemies and deploying their forces accordingly. Economic and trade policies and the use of resources are heavily skewed in the North's favour. And the one central lesson of the Cold War from the major northern powers has been that if you do not have any military clout, why should they take any notice of you? Is it surprising, then, that many in the South are not willing to demilitarize or that some want to become regional superpowers in their own right? Control of militarization cannot be imposed on the South while being ignored within the North. Arms control, disarmament and the curbing of the arms trade cannot and will not become global trends unless the heavily militarized North is a willing party to the process.

To avoid resource conflicts means seeing issues in terms of global security and equitable distribution of wealth and not narrow accounting terms of profit and return on capital. Thus changed policies in the North covering, for example, energy conservation and alternative energy sources in the North to reduce consumption, and technology transfer of minimal polluting and efficient use techniques to the South, are likely to minimize the risk of such conflicts. Renewable energy R&D, and its serious application, then, is a security priority to minimize prospects of conflicts over non-renewable energy reserves.

Another set of questions concerns how our new vision linking development, environment and peace relates to the short-, medium- and long-term aspects of security. Answers may be different in different places and require trade-offs which may hurt some in society, who may resist unless society buffers those losers and helps them redeploy. How should we move to a minimal level of spending on the military, and just what should that spending be? What opportunities arise for conversion – in Africa, for example, with no major military industries there is a great opportunity – and how will that be pursued? What institutions are needed for real security and at what levels? These institutions may have to deal with local and national conflicts involving freelance political and military leaders: does this require new conflict management and peacekeeping systems under a UN banner? Major reforms of the international financial and trade institutions – such as the IMF, World Bank and GATT – will be required to get them to play their part, as well as an enforceable legal system with clear rights and obligations.

Actions are, of course, needed at different levels – local, regional, national and international.

Local

Changing our understanding of security begins in the community where we live, in the work that we do, in our schools, shops, offices, factories and homes. Conflict resolution begins in the home, between child and parent, between partners living together. It starts with people where they are and through them engaging in where they, their children and their children's children want to be. The many voluntary community groups, environmental, peace and development groups have a great role to play in empowering citizens to have their say in security. Now is the time for a citizens' inquiry into security in local communities in every country throughout the world, for the aim of security is to meet needs, not just those of the rich and powerful but of all, including the poor and powerless.

In Canada in the early 1990s, a range of groups organized meetings throughout the country to gauge what people felt their real security needs were. A Security 2000 citizens' enquiry is being discussed by various voluntary groups in Britain for 1995 – a year full of major anniversaries such as the founding of the UN and end of the Second World War. The essential point is that there is an opportunity for ordinary people to be involved in asking and debating the question: what does real security mean for you – locally, as a citizen of your country, as a member of a larger regional grouping, such as the EU or NAFTA, and as a citizen of one world? And what does real security mean for your hopes and fears? How will you try and do things differently in your local community to reach these goals and, finally, what kind of issues and policies should governments and others be working on to ensure security?

We need to be heard and to be active and such an activity is part of meeting what Max-Neef defines as our need for understanding. Feeding this need means being curious, critically conscious and undertaking the investigation, experimentation, analysis, mediation and interpretation that produces the various tools we associate with education, such as books. A citizens' enquiry promotes interactions in the various local institutions through which we can educate ourselves – and our schools, colleges, communities and families.

A shift in emphasis in security from military to the other aspects of security will produce new national budgetary priorities and restructurings. But these will have local effects. For them to be acceptable, provision is needed within communities at local levels for the retraining, redeployment and assistance needed to people affected by the transition – although the same is true for other industries that have seen their markets disappear or decline. That is more likely in communities engaged in understanding their real security needs.

National

The whole of national politics and policies need to be reviewed with a real security perspective – not simply from a narrow, military-based defence review. Changes will be required in both domestic and foreign policy, as Ben Jackson has shown for the UK. A move to a minimal military posture, based on common security and with military forces expected to contribute to peacekeeping through UN operations, would require some retraining of officers and men to fit them for such work.

It also requires a redefinition of the national interest to meet the challenges of the rich/poor divide and environmental threats. Assumptions about 'our interests' – be they American, European or Japanese – cannot, in a real security framework, be based on the right to use whatever resources nations desire wherever they are found. More give, and less material take, will be needed in the North and policies that produce a wider range of satisfiers of the range of human needs than economic goods can provide.

National arms registers, conversion policies and programmes will be required but also policies that conserve and promote renewable sources of energy and materials, debt cancellation and aid policies that create space for developing countries to meet the material needs of their people, and comprehensive trade reform to counter 40 years of the North–South trade trap.[3]

Regional

A range of supranational groups is developing in the world, which could become not mere competing blocks but warring blocks. However, where they embrace former enemies, as in Europe, they offer real prospects of cutting military expenditure greatly, and directing the resources released into other aspects of human security.

Interchange between people in the different states and among those who are often portrayed as enemies can begin to break down the ignorance that can be turned into fear of the enemy by vested interests for their own ends. This is unlikely to be volunteered by leaders at the top, rather it must be pressed for from below. There is, for example, little sign of the radical thinking needed among the rich, as exemplified by the Group of Seven in their summits, that they have even started asking the right questions for real security.

International

The way the UN and its institutions are reformed by the world's governments will set the scene for the international dimension of the move to real security. The challenge is to establish an enabling system in which people can achieve justice. The trend, unfortunately, is one towards a world dominated by large transnational institutions, mostly private corporations but some public, such as the World Bank and IMF. These are increasingly pitting poor people in the South against poor people in the North and may lead to a shift in the North–South axis from being simply geographical to being a certain class of people with the wealth, power and control over resources, located mainly in the North but with a growing minority in the South, serving their interests against the poor and marginalized, North and South.[4] But this is not yet a monolithic world and their interests are not all the same. Where will the conflicts of interest between them take us? How does militarism, which has been an essentially state controlled enterprise, fit into this future – will it, too, become privatized?

Effective, democratic international institutions will be needed to monitor, regulate and control the activities of transnational actors so they contribute to real security. Here the UN is central. The UN Charter begins 'We the peoples' (see Figure 6.1) but it is run and misrun by governments. However it is the only global institution we have with the potential to deal with the vast range of global challenges to humanity. It is only likely to be restructured in ways beneficial to humankind through people-pressure on governments worldwide for a reform of the UN to meet the needs of our individual and collective security. This includes jettisoning the old Roman dictum 'if you want peace, prepare for war' and replacing it with 'if you want peace, prepare for peace', as Michael Renner of the Worldwatch Institute argues.[5] He points out that 'The $8.3 billion that the United Nations spent on peacekeeping from 1948 to 1992 is a trifling fraction – less than three one-hundredths of one per cent – of the roughly $30 trillion devoted to traditional military purposes over the same period'.[6] As part of the development of an alternative, non-violent system for the settlement of conflicts he calls for:

- a shift from offensive weapons and strategies to ones that can defend but not attack; and
- strengthening international peacekeeping and peacemaking capacity.

To achieve this second goal, a reinvigorated UN is required which, he suggests:

- manages an arms transfer register and oversees progressive disarmament with strict limits on military arsenals;

WE THE PEOPLES
OF THE UNITED NATIONS
DETERMINED

to save succeeding generations from the scourge of war, which twice in our lifetimes has brought untold sorrow to mankind, and

to reaffirm faith in fundamental human rights, in the dignity and worth of the human person, in the equal rights of men and women and of nations large and small, and

to establish conditions under which justice and respect for the obligations arising from treaties and other sources of international law can be maintained, and

to promote social progress and better standards of life in larger freedom

AND FOR THESE ENDS

to practice tolerance and live together in peace with one another as good neighbors, and

to unite our strength to maintain international peace and security, and

to ensure, by the acceptance of principles and the institution of methods, that armed force shall not be used, save in the common interest, and

to employ international machinery for the promotion of the economic and social advancement of all peoples,

HAVE RESOLVED TO
COMBINE OUR EFFORTS TO
ACCOMPLISH THESE AIMS.

Figure 6.1 The beginning of the charter of the UN

- runs a 'well-endowed and competently staffed international disarmament verification agency';
- has a trained peacekeeping force at its disposal, with adequate funding, with peace academies studying successes and failures in mediation, devising new methods for peaceful conflict resolution and providing training. This could be backed up by a second line

peacemaking force, with the military capability to deter aggression and enforce cease-fire agreements;
- a reformed security council, representative of the world's population and contribution to the UN, without vetoes and with two-thirds majority voting powers;
- a second chamber to the government representative General Assembly of the UN – a 'world citizens assembly' – with the UN defending individual human rights on security.

Whatever ways are sought, and these are just one set of proposals, the aim is to make the UN the first, and routine, recourse for peacemaking. Despite its apparent distance from the local community, success in this could affect poor people from Bosnia to Somalia, and throughout the world.

RESEARCHERS AND CAMPAIGNERS

At each of these levels, we have to ask if the existing institutions, policy instruments and information are sufficient to meet our human needs and our real security requirements. Here researchers and campaigners could play a major role in the mobilization for action.

The responsibility of researchers, whether in universities and colleges, in industry, think-tanks, governments or pressure groups, is immense. All too often, the most inquiring of minds is constrained by academic norms, and passively fails to engage in any independent analysis of the issues facing the human community, content instead to operate within those narrow intellectual limits considered acceptable. Yet there is a fundamental responsibility for the researcher to question this accepted 'wisdom', which is so often moribund, and instead seek to develop a critical analysis of our predicament and explore creative alternatives.

Just as important is the need for interdisciplinary study. Usually the issues of development, environment and security are perceived as quite separate, whereas, as we have seen, the interconnections are crucial if we are to have any real chance of understanding and countering our predicament.

The researcher has, furthermore, to seek every means to communicate with the human community at large, not least the campaigning and policy-forming groups active in trying to create a genuine new world order. In doing so, the wider community will be informed, and thereby empowered to make a far more effective contribution to changing attitudes and policies.

Campaigning groups from a wide range of areas – such as peace, development, environment – have a major role to play in promoting both public discussion and pressing for action. But their role goes beyond that, for they are at least debating issues at what we might call the right end of the spectrum when so many political 'leaders' are off at the other end fighting over nuances of policies that are likely to lead us further down a confrontational path.

The immense challenge for public interest groups is to take some time out from each one's specific, individual interest to see how they relate to a broader picture of human security and the means of achieving it. Of how it challenges the consumer ideology emerging in the world which dooms the majority to the role of jealous spectators. Campaigning groups that simply continue along lines that reflect essentially a capitalist division of protest, with a niche for every conscience, will diminish their power and impact. However, if they operate as a range of people in different groups but with a broad shared vision working together towards it, they will reinforce each other and move the whole debate, policy process and actions to their end of the spectrum. Undoubtedly arguments over particular priorities will remain, but at least they will be within a real human security framework.

CHOICE AND ACTION

Any attempt to redress inequalities in an environmentally-constrained world will be seen, to a considerable extent, as a threat to the security of the rich and powerful. At the same time, any attempt by them to maintain the *status quo* through military and other means is fundamentally self-defeating. The global system is too integrated and environmentally constrained to continue to permit a minority of the population to live in secure isolation from the majority for ever.

Action to produce a peaceful and stable planetary system is aided by the extensive intellectual and practical efforts over the past two decades aimed at integrating our understanding of development and environmental processes. However, this integration still has to be extended to incorporate an understanding of processes of international security and the dangers of applying those processes as an answer to

North/South polarization. There is an urgent need to do this, and to do so in a truly global context.

We might expect or hope for action by four broad groups or interests. The first is the governments of the major northern states. Sadly, there is little or no sign of political wisdom coming from these quarters at present, and our hopes of leadership from these states would be best discounted, at least in the short term. Although there is little sign from western governments yet, it is possible. It was, after all, the Gorbachev leadership in the former Soviet Union that produced a radical set of policies built on much background work over many years. In other Eastern European states, people pressure played a much greater role.

The second is governments and leaderships in the South, where, once again, wisdom and vision are desperately needed. There are some signs of hope here, especially with the steady evolution of the Group of 15, but previous experience of disunity in the Group of 77 and the Non-Aligned Movement should remind us of the problems of getting effective action. Even so, the activities of just a few states can be positive and, by speaking with a voice which breaks the already stagnant paradigm of the new world order, an impact might just possibly be had on the more powerful states of the North.

The other two groups are those researchers and ngos in the South and in the North which are working towards the common agenda of a peaceful global environment for development. They can form a common thread of concern across the world, can evolve a shared vision of what might be achieved and push for change to achieve this vision, while warning of the violent and unstable alternatives. Ultimately, they must make common cause with governments and international organizations who will eventually come to recognize the need for changes in attitudes and in the very structures of power as the present world 'order' becomes increasingly unworkable. Their present role is, to an extent, a prophetic role, in the sense of 'foretelling the possible' and putting into practice whatever elements of real security they can wherever they can. It is the process of bringing forward the ideal of a more peaceful and stable world and making that ideal an early reality.

References

A JUNGLE FULL OF SNAKES? POWER, POVERTY AND INTERNATIONAL SECURITY

1. See SIPRI (1993) *Arms and Disarmament 1993,* Yearbook of the Stockholm International Peace Research Institute, OUP, Oxford
2. Statement by James Woolsey at Senate Hearings, Washington DC, February 1993
3. This paper draws on two recent publications:
    (a) Rogers, P (1993) *Global Security After the Cold War,* Sheffield Papers in International Studies no 17, University of Sheffield
    (b) Rogers, P and Dando, M (1992) *A Violent Peace: Global Security After the Cold War,* Brasseys, London
4. *World Declaration and Plan of Action for Nutrition,* International Conference on Nutrition, Rome, December 1992, para 1, Plan of Action
5. Tom Whiston 'Global Rotting' *Times Higher Education Supplement,* 1 October 1993, p 18
6. Newbould, Palmer (1974) 'The Global Ecosystem' chapter in *Human Ecology and World Development,* Vann, A and Rogers, P (eds), Plenum Press, London
7. Brooks, E (1974) 'The Implications of Ecological Limits to Development in Terms of Expectations and Aspirations in Developed and Less Developed Countries' chapter in *Human Ecology and World Development,* ref 6
8. Byron John L (1990) 'A New Target for the Submarine Force' *Proceedings of the US Naval Institute,* January, pp 36–39
9. Strategic Advisory Group of the Joint Strategic Target Planning Staff, US Strategic Air Command, 'The Role of Nuclear Weapons in the New World Order' reported in *Navy News and Undersea Technology,* 13 January 1992, Washington DC
10. Barnett, Roger W (1992) 'Regional Conflict: Requires Naval Forces' *Proceedings of the US Naval Institute,* June, pp 28–33
11. Rogers, P (1992) 'A Bomb to Bash the Bullies' *The Guardian,* London, 2 July 1992
12. Kyle, John (1993) 'Commentary: Pursue Global Protection' *Defense News,* May, 1993

References

13. 'Third World Missile Forces' *For Your Eyes Only*, Washington DC, 10 May 1993
14. Leopold, George and Opall, Barbara (1992) 'US, Russia Push Global Protection Plan' *Defense News*, 23 November, p 3
15. Henderson, Breck W (1993) 'Lockheed Wins $689-million Theatre Defense Contract' *Aviation Week and Space Technology*, 21 September, pp 59–60
16. 'Cruise Missiles Becoming Top Proliferation Threat' *Aviation Week and Space Technology*, 1 February 1993, pp 26–7
17. ibid
18. Fulghum, David A (1993) 'US Developing Plan to Down Cruise Missiles' *Aviation Week and Space Technology*, 22 March, pp 46–7
19. Rogers, Paul (1988) *Guide to Nuclear Weapons,* Berg Press, Oxford
20. Fulghum, David A (1993) 'ALCMs Given Nonlethal Role' *Aviation Week and Space Technology*, 22 February, pp 20–22
21. Fulghum, David A (1993) 'Loh Outlines Bomber Plans' *Aviation Week and Space Technology*, 5 July, pp 26–28
22. Munro, Neil (1993) 'Demonstrations Propel USAF Weapon Efforts' *Defense News*, 5 July, p 8
23. Fulghum, David A (1993) 'New Missile Threats Drive EF-111 Program' *Aviation Week and Space Technology*, 10 May, pp 24–25
24. Canan, James W (1993) 'Expeditionary Force' *Air Force Magazine*, June, pp 20–25
25. Ochmanek, David and Bordeaux, John (1993) 'The Lion's Share of Power Projection' *Air Force Magazine*, June, pp 38–42
26. The development of force projection is examined more fully in Rogers, P and Dando, M (1992) *A Violent Peace: Global Security After the Cold War,* Brasseys, London
27. Watkins, Admiral James D (1986) 'The Maritime Strategy' special supplement to the *Proceedings of the US Naval Institute,* January
28. O'Keefe, Sean *et al* (1992) '...From the Sea – Preparing the Naval Service for the 21st Century' *Proceedings of the US Naval Institute*, November, pp 93–96
29. ibid
30. Cushman, John H (1993) 'Maneuver... From the Sea' *Proceedings of the US Naval Institute*, April, pp 47–48
31. Quoted in *Defense News*, 28 June 1993
32. Morrocco, John D (1993) 'US Navy Reorients to Coastal Warfare' *Aviation Week and Space Technology*, 22 March, pp 56–57
33. Lawrence, W P (1993) 'Can Land-Based Bombers Replace Aircraft Carriers?' *Proceedings of the US Naval Institute*, June, pp 12–13
34. Munro, Neil and Opall, Barbara (1992) 'Army, Navy Challenge USAF Strike Mission' *Defense News*, 23 November, p 4
35. 'New Technologies Required for Special Operations' *Tactical Technology*, 12 May 1993

36. ibid
37. As one example of the developing ideas on the economics of sustainable development, see Ekins, Paul and Max-Neef, Manfred (eds) (1992) *Real Life Economics, Understanding Wealth Creation* Routledge, London

CONFLICT AND DEVELOPMENT: WHAT KINDS OF POLICIES CAN REDUCE THE DAMAGING IMPACT OF WAR?

1. For a more detailed discussion of this see Frances Stewart (1993) 'War and underdevelopment: can economic analysis help reduce the costs?' *Journal of International Development Studies*, vol 5, no 4, pp 357–380. This includes many references to the literature in this area. See especially:
   Boothby (1990) 'Working in the war zone: a look at psychological theory and practice in the field' *Mind and Human Interaction*, vol 2, no 2
   Dodge, C and Ranadalea, M (1991) *Reaching Children in War,* Sigma Forlag, Bergen
   Green, R (1992) 'Conflict, food and famine, reflections on sub-Saharan Africa' in Petty *et al* (eds), *Conflict and Relief in Contemporary African Famines* (mimeo), Save the Children Fund and London School of Hygiene and Tropical Medicine, London
   Keynes, J M (1939) 'Paying for the war' *The Times*, 14 and 15 November 1939, reprinted in Moggridge, D (ed) (1978) *The Collected Writing of John Maynard Keynes*, vol XXII, Macmillan, London
   Lake, A *et al* (1990) *After the Wars,* ODC Policy Perspectives no 16, ODC, Washington
   Sen, A K (1981) *Poverty and Famines: an Essay on Entitlement and Deprivation,* Clarendon Press, Oxford
   Watson, T (1991) 'Humanitarianism and war: learning the lessons from recent armed conflicts' Occasional Paper 8, Institute for International Studies, London
   Zwi, A and Ugalde, A (1989) 'Towards an epidemiology of political violence in the Third World' *Soc. Sci. Med.* vol 28, no 7, pp 633–642
2. For further exploration of the issues discussed in this Mozambique case study see:
   Green, R H (1993) 'The Four Horsemen Ride Together: scorched fields of war in Southern Africa' *Journal of Refugee Studies*, forthcoming
   Hanlon, J (1991) *Mozambique: Who Calls the Shots?,* James Currey, London
   Hermele, K (1992) *Mozambican Crossroads: economics and politics in the era of structural adjustment,* Chr Michelsen Institute, Norway
   Nunes, J (1992) *Peasants and Survival: the social consequences of displacement* unpublished report for SIDA, Maputo, Mozambique
   Wilson, K B (1991) 'The New Missionaries' review of J Hanlon

References

Mozambique: Who Calls the Shots? in *Southern African Review of Books,* no 11,
July/October 1991

Wilson, K B (1992) *Internally Displaced, Refugees and Returnees in and from
Mozambique,* SIDA Studies in Emergencies and Disaster Relief, no 1,
Stockholm, Sweden

Wilson, K B (1992) 'Relief and Livelihoods in War Zones in Africa'
pp 1–3 *Development Research Insights,* ODI/IDS, Brighton

Wilson, K B with Nunes, J (1993) 'Repatriation to Mozambique: refugee
initiative and agency planning: the case of Milange District, 1982–1991'
in Allen, T and Morsink, H (eds) (forthcoming 1994) *When Refugees Go
Home: African Experiences,* James Currey, London and Africa World
Press, Trenton NJ

THE DEVELOPMENT TRAP: MILITARISM, ENVIRONMENTAL DEGRADATION AND POVERTY IN THE SOUTH.

1. Sometimes also called Third World, less-developed or underdeveloped
countries.
2. See Deger, Saadet (1986) *Military Expenditure in the Third World Countries:
The Economic Effects,* Routledge and Kegan Paul, London; and Ball, Nicole
(1988) *Security and the Economy in the Third World,* Adamantine Press,
London
3. For example see Myers, Norman (1989) 'Environment and Security'
Foreign Policy, vol 74, spring, pp 23–41, especially p 25
4. World Bank, *World Development Report 1990,* Oxford University Press,
Oxford p 7. Table 2.1 on p 29 shows the distribution of poor by regions
around the world in 1985
5. United States Arms Control and Disarmament Agency (1990) *World
Military Expenditures and Arms Transfers 1989,* US Government Printing
Office, Washington DC
6. Deger, Saadet (1991) 'World Military Expenditure' in SIPRI Yearbook
World Armament and Disarmament 1991, OUP, pp 115–35, provides a
recent survey on the trends of world military spending
7. Mohammed, N A L (1992) *'Military Expenditure in Sub-Saharan Africa: A
Comparative Analysis and Case Study of the Sudan',* PhD Dissertation,
Cambridge University, and Mohammed, N A L (1993) 'Militarization in
Sudan: Trends and Determinants' *Armed Forces & Society,* vol 19, no 3,
deal with the frequency of military coups and the size of the armed forces
in Africa
8. Wolpin, Miles D (1986) *Militarization, Internal Repression and Social Welfare in
the Third World,* Croom Helm, London
9. Mohammed, N A L (1989) 'Environmental Degradation is a Result of

125

Poverty: Rapid Growth is therefore Needed for the Protection of the Environment in the LDCs?' mimeograph, University of Cambridge, p 3

10. Hardoy, Jorge & Satterthwaite, David (1985) 'Third World Cities and the Environment of Poverty' ch 7, pp 171–210, in Repetto, Robert (ed) (1985) *The Global Possible: Resources, Development and New Century,*Yale University Press, London, point to the effect of this migration on the internal (home) environment, cities, and regions' environments

11. UNEP (1975) 'The Proposed Programme' (UNEP/GC / 3), Nairobi, para 100

12. The World Commission on Environment and Development (1987) *Our Common Future,* OUP, Oxford, p 45

13. See, for example, Benoit, Emile (1978) 'Growth and Defence in Developing Countries' *Economic Development & Cultural Change*, vol 26, no 2, pp 271–80; and Janowitz, M (1964) *The Military in the Political Development of New Nations,* Phoenix Books, London

14. Most LDCs and particularly African countries have volunteer armies. See Ball, ref 2, p 308, Figure 8-1

15. Deger, Saadet & Smith, Ron (1985) 'Military Expenditure and Development: The Economic Linkages' *IDS Bulletin*, vol 16, no 4, pp 49–54 argue that the government expenditure in LDCs equals the finance which is available from tax revenues, domestic borrowing, money creation and foreign aid. This inelastic function sets an upper limit on the budget allocations

16. See Ball, ref 2, p 323

17. Harris, G, Kelly, M & Pranowo (1988) 'Trade-offs Between Defence and Education/Health Expenditures in Developing Countries' *Journal of Peace Research*, vol 25, no 2, pp 165–77. However, in a sample of 26 African countries for the period 1967–1976, Nabe, Omar (1983) 'Military Expenditures and Industrialization in Africa' *Journal of Economic Issues*, vol 17, no 2, pp 575–87, concludes that military expenditure impeded social development efforts in education in these countries

18. Ibid refs 15–17

19. See Mohammed (1992) '*Military Expenditure in Sub-Saharan Africa: A Comparative Analysis and Case Study of the Sudan*', PhD Dissertation, Cambridge University and Deger (1986) in *Military Expenditure in the Third World Countries: The Economic Effects,* Routledge and Kegan Paul, London, pp 87–8

20. Brzoska, M (1983) 'Research Communication: The Military Related External Debt of Third World Countries' *Journal of Peace Research*, vol 20, no 3, pp 271–7

21. Hess, P (1989) 'Force Ratios, Arms Imports and Foreign Aid Receipts in the Developing Nations' *Journal of Peace Research*, vol 26, no 4, pp 399–412 found that arms imports had a significant positive impact on receipts of foreign aid in a sample of 76 LDCs for the period 1978–1984. However, this depended on the composition of nations in the sample. The

significance of arms imports vanished when the Middle Eastern countries were omitted from the sample

22. Eleazu, U O (1973) 'The Role of the Army in African Politics: a Reconsideration of Existing Theories and Practices' *The Journal of Developing Areas*, vol 7, no 2, pp 265–286

23. See Benoit, Emile (1978) 'Growth and Defence in Developing Countries' *Economic Development and Cultural Change*, vol 26, no 2

24. For example, see Deger (1986) in *Military Expenditure in the Third World Countries: The Economic Effects,* Routledge and Kegan Paul, London, pp 87–8; Deger, Saadet & Smith, Ron (1983) 'Military Expenditure and Growth in less Developed Countries' *Journal of Conflict Resolution*, vol 27, no 2, pp 335–53; and Faini, R, Annez, P & Taylor, L (1984) 'Defense Spending, Economic Structure, and Growth: Evidence Among Countries and Over Time' *Economic Development & Cultural Change*, vol 32, no 3, pp 487–98 for empirical evidence. This is reviewed in detail in Mohammed, ref 7

25. Smith, D & Smith, Ron (1980) 'Military Expenditure, Resources and Development' *Birkbeck College Discussion Paper no 87*, University of London

26. See Nabe, ref 17

27. Gyimah-Brempong, K (1989) 'Defense Spending and Economic Growth in SubSaharan Africa: An Econometric Investigation' *Journal of Peace Research*, vol 26, no 1, pp 79–90

28. Mohammed, N A L (1993) 'Defence Spending and Economic Growth in Sub-Saharan Africa: Comment on Gyimah-Brempong' *Journal of Peace Research*, vol 30, no 1, pp 95–97 and Mohammed, NAL (1993) 'Defence Spending and Economic Growth in Sub-Saharan Africa: A Rejoinder' *Journal of Peace Research*, vol 30, no 1, p 99

29. See also Scheetz, T (1991) 'The Macroeconomic Impact of Defence Expenditures: Some Econometric Evidence for Argentina, Chile, Paraguay and Peru' *Defence Economics*, vol 3, no 1, pp 65–81

30. Looney, E Robert (1986) 'Austerity and Military Expenditures in Developing Countries: The Case Study of Venezuela' *Socio-Economic Planning Sciences*, vol 20, no 3, pp 161–4

31. For example, Verner, J G (1983) 'Budgetary Trade-Offs Between Education and Defense in Latin America: A Research Note' *Journal of Developing Areas*, vol 18, no 1, pp 77–92. Another example of a study on warfare-welfare trade-offs is Dixon, W J & Moon, B E (1986) 'The Military Burden and Basic Human Needs' *Journal of Conflict Resolution*, vol 30, no 4, pp 660–84. They found that when controlling for the size of the military establishment, military spending tends to inhibit welfare outcomes in LDCs

32. For a discussion of the developmental effects of Third World armies, see Benoit, ref 13, and Ball, ref 2

33. Homer-Dixon, Thomas F (1990) 'Environmental Change and Violent

Conflict' *Occasional paper no 4*, International Security Studies Program, American Academy of Arts and Sciences, Cambridge, Massachusetts, US See also Atles, E J Karthals (1992) 'The Arms Race, Development and the Environment in Peacetime' pp 65–79, and Gamba-Stonehouse, Virginia (1992) 'Environmental Crises: Cause or Consequence of International Conflict?' pp 101–113, both in Gleditsch, Nils Petter (ed) (1992) 'Conversion and the Environment, Proceedings of a Seminar in Perm, Russia, 24-27 November, 1991' *International Peace Research Institute, Oslo, PRIO Report no 2*, May 1992, and Westing, Arthur H (1989) 'The Environmental Component of Comprehensive Security' *Bulletin of Peace Proposals*, vol 20, no 2, pp 129–134

34. See Ball, ref 2 and Maizels, A & Nissanke, M K (1986) 'The Determinants of Military Expenditures in Developing Countries' *World Development*, vol 14, no 9, pp 1125–40

35. See Brauer, Jurgen 'Arms Production in Developing Nations: the Relation to Industrial Structure, Industrial Diversification and Human Capital Formation' *Defence Economics*, vol 2, no 2, 1991, pp 165–176 for the recent trend of arms production in the Third World

36. See Atles, ref 33, p 71

37. Chourci, N (1992) 'Natural Resources and Conflict: The Need for Confidence-Building and Crisis Management. Environment and Conflict: New principles For Environmental Conduct' *Disarmament*, vol 15, no 1, pp 67–78

38. Of which 59% are in uniform. See Westing, Arthur H (1988) 'The Military Sector vis-a-vis the Environment' *Journal of Peace Research*, vol 25, no 3, pp 257–264

39. Ibid

40. Cookson, Clive 'War Worsens the Spread of Aids in Africa', *Financial Times*, 27 August 1992

41. See Westing, ref 33, p 129

42. See ref 12, p 290

43. See Gamba-Stonehouse, ref 33, p 102. Gleick, P (1990) 'Environment, Resources and Security; Arenas for Conflict, Areas for Cooperation' *Plenary Address to the 40th Pugwash Conference*, 19 September 1990, UK provides many examples of how resources have been used as strategic goals, have been targets during conflict, and have been tools of war

44. Deger, Saadet, & Sen, Somnath (1992) 'Reorientation and Conversion of Military R&D towards Environmental R&D and protection' pp 165–194, in Gleditsch (ed) ref 33. See also Westing, ref 33 for the regional threats of water pollution

45. Starr, Joyce R (1991) 'Water Wars' *Foreign Policy*, no 82, pp 17–36, reviews conflicts emanating from water competition, with special emphasis on the Middle East. See also Lodgaard, Sverre (1992) 'Environmental Security, World Order, and Environmental Conflict Resolution' pp 115–136, in Gleditsch (ed) ref 33

46. See Gamba-Stonehouse, ref 33, p 109. Homer-Dixon, ref 33, p 3 also shows the effect of environmental factors on the conflict over the Euphrates river and on the internal conflict in the Philippines
47. Quoted in Myers, ref 3, p 32
48. See ref 12, p 7
49. See Homer-Dixon, ref 33, for an excellent theoretical discussion of the causal links between environmental change and conflict
50. *Conversion–Opportunities for Development and Environment: The Process of Transition from Military to Civilian Economies,* International Conference, 24–27 February 1992, Dortmund, Germany, Conference Report, p 8
51. See the World Bank, *World Development Report 1990,* ref 4, and Hassan, Shaukat (1991) 'Environmental Sources of Conflict in the South Asian Subcontinent' *Disarmament,* vol 15, no 1, pp 79–95 for some recommended measures to eliminate poverty
52. Gleditsch, Nils Petter & Molvaer, Reidulf (1992) 'Introduction: Conversion and the Environment' pp 1–19, in Gleditsch (ed), ref 33
53. Dunne, Paul & Willett, Susan 'The Economics of Conversion in the United Kingdom' paper presented to UN Conference on *Conversion – Opportunities for Development and Environment,* Dortmund, 24–27 February 1992
54. Batchelor, Peter & Mohammed, Nadir 'Demilitarization and Conversion in Africa' paper presented to the *Conference of Socialist Economists,* London, 10–13 July 1992
55. Kaldor, M 'Problems of Adjustment of Lower Levels of Military Spending in Developed and Developing Countries', paper prepared for World Bank Conference, Washington DC, 25–26 April, 1991
56. See ref 53
57. Gleditsch, ref 33, p 32
58. Perelet, Renat (1992) 'Environmentally Sound Conversion: International Experience' pp 231–242, in Gleditsch (ed), ref 33, gives many examples of making effective use of military products, facilities and personnel. Examples could be the use of military satellites for environmental monitoring, or troops for eliminating negative consequences of technological accidents
59. See ref 50, p 22
60. See refs 54 & 55
61. See also ref 53
62. Crongberg, Tarja (1992) 'The Social Construction of Military Technology: With Special Reference to the Environment' pp 139–164, in Gleditsch (ed), ref 33, that whole volume; ref 53; Barker, Terry, Dunne, Paul & Smith, Ron (1991) 'Measuring the Peace Dividend in the United Kingdom' *Journal of Peace Research,* vol 28, no 4, pp 345–358; and Dunne, Paul (1991) 'Conversion and Employment: a Comparative Assessment' *DAE Working Paper no 9116,* University of Cambridge, for further discussion of the issues associated with conversion

MILITARISM, THE UK ECONOMY AND CONVERSION POLICIES IN THE NORTH

1. Vagts, A (1959) *A History of Militarism, Civilian and Military,* Hollis and Carter, London
2. Shaw, M (1991) *Post Military Society – Militarism, Demilitarisation and War at the end of the Twentieth Century,* Polity Press, Cambridge, pp 9–15
3. Barnett, C (1986) *The Audit of War: The Illusion and Reality of Britain as a Great Power,* Macmillan, London
4. Edgerton, D (1991) *England and the Aeroplane – An Essay on a Militant and Technological Nation,* Macmillan, London, p 65
5. Ibid, p 82
6. Ibid, p 88
7. Hogan, M J (1987) *The Marshall Plan, America, Britain and the Reconstruction of W Europe,* Cambridge University Press, London, p 380
8. Science Policy Study Group (1991) *Future Relations Between Defence and Civil Science and Technology,* SPSG, London, p 1
9. Project on Demilitarization (1993) *Militarism or Disarmament? Challenging the West's Technological Arms Race,* Prodem, Leeds, p 1
10. Ricardo, D (1973) *The Principles of Political Economy and Taxation,* J M Petit and Sons, London, pp 160–61
11. Tate, M (1971) *The Disarmament Illusion:The Movement for the Limitations of Armaments to 1907,* Russell & Russell, London, p 12
12. Mosley, H (1984) *The Arms Race, Economic and Social Consequences,* Lexington Books, Lexington, US, p 9
13. Ibid, p 12
14. See, for example, Chalmers, M (1985) *Paying for Defence, Military Spending and British Decline,* Pluto Press, London, and Melman, S (1974) *The Permanent War Economy: American Capitalism in Decline,* Simon and Schuster, New York
15. See Chalmers, ref 14, p 56
16. See Chalmers, ref 14, p 112
17. Benn, T (1974) *Speeches by Tony Benn,* Spokesman Books, London, p 48
18. Coopey, R (forthcoming) 'Restructuring Civil and Military Science and Technology: The Ministry of Technology in the 1960's.' in Coopey *et al* (eds) *Defence Science and Technology, Adjusting to Change,* p 66
19. Ibid, p 75
20. *Statement on the Defence Estimates 1990,* HMSO, Cmnd 1022-I
21. House of Commons Science and Technology Committee, First Report Session 1992–93, *The Policy and Organisation of the Office of Science and Technology,* volume 2, HC 228-II, pp 184–187
22. *Financial Times,* 27 September 1993
23. Deger, S (1993) 'World Military Expenditure' in *SIPRI Yearbook 1993,* OUP, Oxford, p 367

References

24. Cooper, J (1991) *The Soviet Defence Industry – Conversion and Reform*, RIIA/Pinter, London, p 95
25. Cooper, J (1993) *The Conversion of the Former Soviet Defence Industry*, RIIA, Chatham House, London, pp 23–24
26. Ibid, p 33
27. Ibid, p 38
28. *Financial Times*, 12 March 1993
29. *New Economy*, 1993, vol 4, no 1, p 2 National Commission for Economic Conversion and Disarmament, Washington
30. Office of Technology Assessment (1993) *Defence Conversion: Redirecting R&D – Summary*, OTA, Washington, pp 28–29
31. Ibid, p 31
32. *New Economy*, 1992, vol 3, no 4, p 2
33. See ref 30, p 10
34. *The Guardian*, 19 February 1993
35. *UK Defence Statistics 1993*, Ministry of Defence, Table 2.24, p 43
36. Select Committee on Trade and Industry (1993) *British Aerospace Industry* 3rd Report, HC 536-I, Session 1992–93
37. Project on Demilitarization (forthcoming) *Arms Conversion East and West*, Prodem, Leeds
38. European Parliament Committee on Regional Policy (1993) *Regional Impact of the Conversion of the arms industries – Draft report*, p 14
39. See ref 37

PROMOTING REAL SECURITY – IMPLICATIONS FOR POLICY IN THE NORTH

1. This chapter is based on an edited, revised version of *Biting the Bullet: Real Security in a New World*, published by WDM in September 1993
2. Hargreaves, Clare (1992) *Snowfields*, Zed, London
3. *Financial Times*, 6 July 1993
4. *The Times*, 6 July 1993, p 18
5. *Sunday Times*, 11 July 1993
6. SIPRI Yearbook 1993, *Press Summary*, 15 June 1993, p 9. Russia's budget for procuring military equipment fell by 32 per cent in 1991 and 68 per cent in 1992, according to *The Economist*, 28 August 1993. This article also shows the great problems faced by the government in trying to manage such a large and rapid transition.
7. Defending Our Future: Statement on the *Defence Estimates 1993*, cm 2270 HMSO, London, July 1993, p 8
8. *Defence Estimates 1993*, p 77
9. A point noted, for example, in a *Financial Times* leader 'Rethinking British Defence', 10 February 1993

10. Using this group for comparison follows an approach used by Malcolm Chalmers, 'Britain and Alliance Burden-Sharing' in Clarke, Michael and Sabin, Philip (eds) (1993) *British Defence Choices for the Twenty-First Century,* Centre for Defence Studies and Brassey's, London. The average is not weighted according to the economic size of the countries. If the average of all 11 of Britain's EC partners is used for comparison, the national average figure is only slightly higher, at 2.4% of GNP
11. Ref 10, Table 1
12. See ref 9
13. Halliday, Fred (1993) *Sleepwalking through history? The New World and its Discontents,* Discussion Paper 4, The Centre for Global Governance, London School of Economics, London
14. For a disturbing and rigorous critique of intervention in Somalia see African Rights (1992) *Operation Restore Hope: A Preliminary Assessment,* 11 Marshalsea Rd, London SE1 1EP
15. Ref 14, p 53
16. SIPRI (1993) *SIPRI Yearbook 1993,* OUP, Oxford
17. *Good government and the aid programme,* speech by Lynda Chalker at the Royal Institute of International Affairs, 25 June 1991
18. *The Guardian,* 18 February 1993
19. Speech to Royal Institute for International Affairs, (Chatham House), London, 27 January 1993
20. Ref 8, p 45
21. £18.7 million from the MoD. £17.7 million under the UK Military Training Assistance Scheme which brought 367 students from 54 countries to courses in the UK and funded the provision of 115 Loan Service Personnel to 16 countries where some 11,000 military students received training (FCO Departmental Report 1993, p 19)
22. Ref 8, p 52
23. Ref 8, p 74
24. British American Security Information Council (1993) *Showing no restraint: Missed opportunities for arms trade control,* BASIC, London
25. Ref 8, p 74
26. Export Credit Guarantee Department (1993) *Annual Report and Trading Accounts 1991/92,* HMSO, London, p 10
27. Trade and Industry Committee, House of Commons (1992) *Exports to Iraq: Minutes of Evidence, Midland Bank,* HMSO, London, 12 February 1992, p 375
28. Amnesty International British Section (1992) *Repression Trade (UK) Limited: How the UK makes torture and death its business,* London
29. UNDP (1993) *Human Development Report 1993,* OUP, Oxford, Table 3, p 141
30. Ref 29, Table 21, p 177
31. UNICEF (1993) *State of the World's Children Report 1993,* OUP, Oxford, p 50

32. United Nations Fund for Population Activities (1993) *The State of World Population 1993,* UNFPA, New York, p 32
33. Ref 31, p 49
34. Ref 31, p 49
35. UNDP (1992) *Human Development Report 1992,* OUP, Oxford, p 82
36. Ref 6, p 9
37. Quoted in Deger, S and Sen, S (1991) *Arms and a child: A SIPRI report for UNICEF on the impact of military expenditure in Sub-Saharan Africa on the survival, protection and development of children,* UNICEF Staff Working Paper 9, p 33
38. Ref 37, p 38
39. Ref 31, p 50
40. In a speech by then World Bank President Barber Conable, quoted in the *Financial Times,* 27 September 1989
41. Ref 16, p 393
42. Catholic Institute for International Relations (1992) *Brazil: Democracy and development* (Comment series), CIIR, London, p 24
43. George, Susan (1992) *The Debt Boomerang: How Third World Debt Harms us all,* TNI/Pluto, London, p 166
44. CIIR (1993) *Coca, Cocaine and the War on Drugs,* CIIR Comment, London, p 11
45. Lloyds List, 'GATT says free trade can help stifle drugs' 1 April 1993
46. *Financial Times,* 18 July 1991
47. Call, Chuck (1992) *The US drug war in Colombia,* Paper presented to the CIIR seminar, 'Colombia: Prospects for peace and democracy', April 1992, p 1
48. Foreign and Commonwealth Office (1993) *Central America, the Caribbean and Mexico: The fight against drug trafficking,* FCO Background Brief, London
49. *Financial Times,* 12 September 1993
50. *Sunday Express,* 25 March 1990
51. Ref 47, p 12
52. Quoted in ref 47, p 3
53. Quoted in ref 47, p 13
54. MoD (1993) *Defence Statistics 1993,* HMSO, London
55. Barker, Terry, Dunne, Paul and Smith, Ron (1991) 'Measuring the Peace Dividend in the United Kingdom' *Journal of Peace Research,* vol 28, no 4, p 531
56. This last point is particularly stressed in the conclusion of Schofield, Steven, Dando, Malcolm, and Ridge, Michael (1992) *Conversion of the British Defence Industries,* Peace Research Report no 30, Department of Peace Studies, University of Bradford, Bradford, p 85
57. *Financial Times,* 12 March 1993
58. Brett, Bill, Gill, Ken and Todd, Ron (1992) *The new industrial challenge: The need for defence diversification,* Institute of Professionals, Managers and

Specialists (IPMS), Manufacturing, Science, Finance Union (MSF) & Transport and General Workers Union (TGWU), London, p 3

59. TGWU Biennual delegates conference 1993, Composite motion 41, 'Defence and Defence Diversification'
60. McMahon, Will and Williamson, Janet (1993) *Arms Conversion,* Campaign Against the Arms Trade (CAAT), London
61. See Chalmers, Malcolm (1990) *UK Defence Requirements 1990–2000.* Saferworld, Bristol, 1990 and ref 10 for a much more detailed scenario of how personnel and equipment could be scaled down to meet a 50 per cent reduction
62. Public Expenditure Statement, November 1993
63. UNDP (1991) *Human Development Report 1991,* OUP, Oxford, p 81
64. Foreign Affairs Committee Report *Expenditure Plans of FCO and ODA,* July 1993, p 31
65. Projections based on UNICEF, ODA projects
66. Low income countries (those with per capita incomes of less than US$610 in 1990) owe the UK about £4 billion, so an 80% write-off would cost £3.2 billion. (*Hansard,* vol 205, col 169, 4 March 1992)
67. *Financial Times,* 6 November 1992
68. *Hansard,* vol 227, col 87–88, 22 June 1993
69. For a detailed analysis of these issues see Saferworld (1992) *Arms and Duel-Use Exports from the EC: A Common policy for Regulation and Control,* Saferworld, Bristol

CONCLUSION: PROPHETS AND PRACTITIONERS

1. Chambers, R (1983) *Rural Development: Putting the Last First,* Longman, Harlow
2. Max-Neef, Manfred 'Development and human needs' in *Real Life Economics: Understanding Wealth Creation,* Paul Ekins and Manfred Max-Neef (eds) (1993) Routledge, London and New York, pp 194–214
3. See Coote, Belinda (1992) *The Trade Trap – Poverty and the Global Commodity Markets,* Oxfam, Oxford, which looks at the terms of trade between North and South and calls for the development of a fair trading system, and Tim Lang and Colin Hines (1993) *The New Protectionism – Protecting the future against free trade,* Earthscan, London, which calls for sustainable trade that protects the environment and builds on local trade and production rather than unregulated global trade
4. Sklair, Leslie (1991) *Sociology of the Global System,* Harvester Wheatsheaf, New York & London
5. Renner, Michael (1993) *Critical Junctions: The Future of Peacekeeping,* Worldwatch Paper 114, Worldwatch Institute, Washington DC
6. Ref 5, p 29

Index